THE FLY
IN THE
OINTMENT

To my Wonderful
friend & colleague.

Pens Crabtn

2·11·09

THE FLY
IN THE
OINTMENT

WHY DENOMINATIONS AREN'T HELPING THEIR CONGREGATIONS . . . AND HOW THEY CAN

J. RUSSELL CRABTREE

CHURCH PUBLISHING
New York

Library of Congress Cataloging-in-Publication Data

Crabtree, J. Russell, 1950-
   The fly in the ointment : why denominations aren't helping their churches–
and how they can / by J. Russell Crabtree.
      p.   cm.
   Includes bibliographical references.
   ISBN 978-0-89869-606-6 (pbk.)
   1. Christian sects. 2. Christian union. 3. Change – Religious aspects –
Christianity. 4. Church renewal. 5. Church growth. 6. Church attendance.
I. Title.
BR157.C73 2008
262–dc22

                                                                2008033785

Church Publishing Incorporated
445 Fifth Avenue
New York, NY 10016
www.churchpublishing.org

5 4 3 2 1

To David Lee Maze
SP4-E4 Army Selective Service

who died in Cambodia
May 28, 1970

to whom I have made promises

Contents

PREFACE

I want to support the view that the foundation of reality itself is a unified, indeterminate maze of possibilities.[1] —Danah Zohar

As a physics student I was always struck with the concept of momentum. Two objects that appear to be identical in photographs are radically different if one has momentum and the other does not. A snapshot taken of a vase in midair obscures the fact that it is actually in freefall and about to be smashed into shards when it hits the floor while another identical vase is sitting on a shelf in a gallery growing in value as it ages.

As a consultant, I look at the statistics of churches and see many churches with 20 persons in worship services. I am struck by the fact that some churches with 20 members today will have a thousand members in five years. Others will be closed. You could take a photograph of two groups of 20 and they would look the same. But hidden by the snapshot is a mysterious momentum that is taking them down very different paths. It is not the number of persons in a church that tells the story. It is the momentum.

I take as the Christian symbol for this book the Cross of St. Andrew. It is based on the tradition that St. Andrew was crucified on a cross in the shape of an X. But it also offers a rich symbol expressing the mystery of momentum. Is the circle at the center of the cross on its way up or down? It could be either. Is a church with 20 persons in worship growing in strength and vitality, or on its way to death? It could be either.

I chose this symbol for another reason. St. Andrew began as a disciple of John the Baptist. When he met Jesus, he realized that his relationship with John had been a preamble to what was to come next. He decided to follow Jesus. At that point of decision, the momentum in his life shifted in another direction. The capacity to embrace that shift makes St. Andrew a symbol of a dynamic life.

The Gospels almost never tell how these kinds of changes actually occur. Were there friends of Andrew that thought he had betrayed the cause? Were there family members that thought he had lost his mind? Did he go through a period of self-doubt and ambivalence? We don't know. All we know is that he embraced the transformation.

The capacity to see one season of your life as preamble to another is the critical factor for healthy change. It does not deny the preciousness of the previous season. But neither does it claim it as destiny. We must not build houses on the Mount of Transfiguration. Transformation requires memory fused with a new context and a heart of discovery.

This book is written in the spirit of St. Andrew and in honor of the Lord who called him. The church as many of us have known it is passing away. As it is falling, it is also rising into new forms. We cannot tell from the snapshot the mystery of its momentum. We only know that Jesus is always the one we want to follow next.

Acknowledgments

It is fair to say that this book has roughly 50,000 contributors. The vast majority of these must remain unnamed because the contribution was an anonymous, though very personal, sharing of their thoughts through a series of questions they agreed to answer. Even though I have never had the pleasure of meeting most of these persons, they never became mere statistics to me. The numbers they coded into their responses are symbols of their stories. Our stories are a significant aspect of our humanity as well as the image of God we all express.

Some of these 50,000 contributors are church members; others are church leaders. Some are engaged with regional associations such as presbyteries, dioceses, synods, conferences, etc. Many are citizens responding with their local public library in mind. For others, it is the arboretum they are thinking about. Still others are staff members reflecting on the quality of their workplace experience.

Many are not anonymous at all. Several thousand have sat in scores of trainings I have conducted on suicide awareness or family violence intervention training. They have brought me their insights and allowed me to practice and expand my own skills at the same time.

These disparate groups of people have a wide range of concerns and perspectives that are distinctive. But they share a common unity in the fact that they are engaged in and with organizations. They have more to teach each other than they often realize. Spiritually, this is because there is "one God and Father of us all who is overall and through all and in all" (Ephesians 4:6). I want to acknowledge and thank all of them for the ripples of blessing that have come to me through their lives and their hopes for a better future.

However, in the midst of a multitude too great to number, a few names are important to mention. I want to thank the Rev. Rebecca McClain and the Rev. Tom Blackmon for carrying the idea for this book to Church Publishing Incorporated and for the support of Davis Perkins and Susan Erdey in getting in published. My dear friend and co-worker Carolyn Weese spent hours reading various iterations of the manuscript, offering invaluable insight and unwavering support. Harvey Weese, often without knowing it, has been a source of strength and encouragement because he simply believes in me. Both offered me a generous hospitality in their home that liberates the spirit to do its best.

The folks at People Management International have also been such an encouragement and I want to mention them: Ed Poff, Rob Stevenson, Mark Stevenson, Suz Grimes, Tony Kroening, Phil Thompson, Kim Burnes, Tim Cox, and Rick Heltne.

My wife, Shawn, has been such an enthusiastic supporter and patient encourager. As a skilled manager herself in a hospital environment, she has had much to teach me and has made many helpful suggestions. Those who offer us spiritual support are also priceless resources for us, especially the Rev. George Glazier of St. Stephen's Episcopal Church and Father Vinny McKiernan of the Newman Center in Columbus, Ohio.

Finally, to the God of the universe who brings such richness to my life and fills my days with wonder, I give my heartfelt thanks.

Introduction

THE FLY IN THE OINTMENT

A supersonic plane reaches a point before its sound does. Imagine arriving at a point and then waiting for the arrival of your own sound. In this context, you are there before the fact. You have created a phenomenon, gotten ahead of it after it was created, and observed it catch up with you.[2]
— Stanley M. Davis

This book has its genesis in a meeting that took place in the early 1990s. In that particular case it was a meeting of presbytery council in the Presbyterian denomination, but it could as easily have been a diocesan standing committee in the Episcopal Church, or a synod council in the Lutheran Church. As a clergy member of the council, I had conducted an analysis of the state of our member congregations and had been granted time on the agenda to present my findings. The first part of the presentation highlighting the decline in membership had nothing new to say that had not been spoken, written, and debated since the mid-1960s when the attrition began. New, however, was the finding that the revenue for most churches in that association would soon drop near the fixed-cost threshold where discretionary funds would evaporate to zero. Because the presbytery is funded from the discretionary money of local churches, this meant that funding for the presbytery would drop precipitously as church after church hit that threshold, and for those fortunate churches that were not approaching that threshold, there were many mission organizations competing with judicatories for those discretionary dollars.

As I closed my presentation, there was an awkward silence, the kind I have since come to recognize as the tipping point between denial and despair. As a church consultant, I have now learned how important it is to give people a way forward when you bring them bad news; if the disease is not terminal, tell them that it is not and provide a remedy. But I was younger then.

1

The silence finally broke and the straw fell in the direction of denial. "Well," spoke a seasoned member of the council with an unblemished Presbyterian pedigree, "I have more faith than that." That ended the conversation. Unfortunately, it didn't avert the funding crisis that was barreling down on that body of leaders, a crisis exacerbated by a controversy that would swirl around the nature of compulsory assessments levied upon local congregations in that particular system. It was a budgetary disaster. The specifics can be put aside. This pattern has been repeated across the nation.

I suppose, on the positive side, my friend's statement signals that denominational agencies, the ones that are supposed to be helping local congregations become vital and effective, still believe in miracles! But it comes at the price of a nearly wholesale abandonment of a reality we do not want to face: denominations are failing their local congregations. The pulse and respiration of our systems are threading toward shutdown and we are conducting business as usual. We keep finding ways not to engage what is happening.

Some Key Thoughts in This Book

The central thrust of this book can be expressed in one sentence: We need to mount a major, nationwide effort to redevelop regional associations to make them transformational organizations. Here is the thread of the argument.

1. *Denominational leaders are sending a confused message to the church regarding the need for change.* Their ambivalent message hinders growth and obscures the depth of the issues that need to be addressed.

2. *The problem we are facing is not a simply numerical decline, but churches where members indicate such poor quality of community life that it is difficult to invite new people into them.* Too few members can clearly deny that they are simply going through the motions. Too few members are clearly satisfied with what is happening in their churches.

3. *The primary obstacle to improvement is that local church leaders do not have the knowledge or insight to know what to do.* They are sounding a clear, unambiguous call for help from their regional bodies as they wrestle with what to do.

4. *Satisfaction levels of church leaders regarding the work of their regional associations is abysmally low, largely because these associations are not providing what they are asking for.* This performance issue appears to be more fundamental and durable than other, more highly publicized issues impacting the church.

5. *Regional associations are not able to provide what local churches need because they do not understand organizational-level dynamics and are functioning with values, skills, and time management that are inappropriate to the regional level.* Realigning regional associations to function at the appropriate organizational level will impact everything from how leaders are selected to how meetings are conducted.

6. *In order to provide what local congregations need, regional associations must be in command of a working strategic menu, and provide effective strategic coaching and leadership development to local church leaders.* Seminaries are not providing the training necessary for transformational leadership; regional associations will have to complete this educational process and include key lay leaders as well.

7. *The redevelopment of regional associations to provide these services will require a major cultural shift in their organizations from a mono-optional perspective to a multi-optional perspective.* This cultural shift, which has been accepted and engaged by nearly every other nonprofit and for-profit organization in the United States, has not yet been accepted in the church.

8. *In order to effectively manage the scarce resources of time and money, regional association leaders must gain greater clarity distinguishing between who they are called to help and who they are called to serve.* When an organization fails to make this distinction, it fails everywhere. It cannot serve its donors, it cannot help its clients, and it cannot manage its bystanders.

9. *As regional associations become clearer about who they are called to serve, they will free up resources for the critical task of providing a comprehensive, strategic resourcing system for local church leaders.* The current services provided for church leaders are generally episodic, piecemeal, and strategically ineffective.

10. *The revenue generation process of regional associations must be recast to match the realities of a competitive market for discretionary*

dollars and demonstrate value added, low overhead, and quality control. This is simply the revenue facet of the cultural shift from a mono-optional to a multi-optional culture.

In making the case for redeveloping regional associations, I take up a point of view that will challenge a number of assumptions, some dearly held. Based upon an alternative reading of the information now at hand we will explore

1. Why wake-up calls addressed to local churches don't wake anyone up.
2. Why it is easier to make the case that a person should get a library card than join a denominational church.
3. How the qualities that make a person effective in their local church may guarantee failure in a regional association role.
4. Why most meetings of regional associations are strategically useless.
5. What elevators have to teach us about why most planning efforts fail.
6. The three top things that people want from their regional associations — and don't want.
7. Why the fastest way to sink an organization is to focus on the people you want to help rather than focusing on the people you are called to serve.
8. The twelve things your pastor did not learn in seminary and needs to know.
9. Why brainstorming can be such a bad idea.
10. Why positive thinking can have such a negative effect.
11. Why you don't want more denominational loyalty in your church.
12. The six reasons people give to anything but not to everything.
13. The important resource regional associations usually penalize by ignoring.

Because this book is based on research findings, it contains tables of numbers. Like crosses and communion tables, the numbers that populate this book are symbols of stories. The symbols tell an often heartbreaking tale of churches that are not simply teetering on the edge of survival; they are teetering on the edge of meaning. Many people in them indicate that they are simply going through the motions; the activity required to keep the doors open has outlived the purpose that opened the doors in the first place. Like voyagers marooned on an island, most have given up hope that representatives from their denomination connectional system will arrive with any meaningful help.

This book ponders the situation and proposes a way forward. The disease is not terminal. There are remedies. But these will require a deep, systemic change in the denominational systems that are called to support congregations. Specifically, we need to begin a conversation about redeveloping regional associations in much the same way we have learned to speak of redeveloping local congregations.

The Research Base

This book is based on 25 years of experience working with organizations, combined with a meta-analysis of several streams of data, some which are statistically compelling and others based on smaller samples that are provocative. More research would be useful in these areas. There appears to be little research conducted on attitudes of local church leaders regarding their regional associations. A call to the research division of the Presbyterian Church USA indicated three surveys on file — only two of which had actually been conducted. A description of the various data streams referred to in this book can be found in Appendix A.

I write this from the perspective of an insider-outsider. On the one hand, I have served as a pastor in the local church and as a leader within a regional association, in my case a presbytery. I have served on councils, chaired divisions, led strategic planning efforts, developed staff rationales, and worked on social justice issues. On the other hand, I have worked with a number of other organizations and have benefited from a healthy dose of extra-ecclesiastical thinking which I also believe is a gift of the Spirit. In general, I observe that denominational systems lag far behind other missional organizations, nonprofit and quasi-nonprofit, in making the changes required to thrive in the world as it currently exists.

A Different Redevelopment Effort:
Transformational Regional Associations

What is needed is a major redevelopment of regional associations. The whole redevelopment effort aimed at local congregations has had some limited success, but was targeted at the wrong level. Unless we have regional associations that are strong enough and skilled enough to coach congregational leaders, any revitalization effort will be difficult to sustain. The redevelopment of regional associations would assemble the kind of system that could support the emergence of vital congregations.

The goal of this redevelopment effort would be to create transformational regional associations. The sole, strategic thrust of transformational regional associations is the enterprise of developing healthy, vital congregations. Creating these regional associations will require more than a vision statement; it will require a total realignment of the system including organizational culture and structure, redefining what leaders value and do, restructuring revenue streams, reallocating resources, reshaping communication process and content — literally, rethinking every aspect of a regional association's life. I am proposing a zero-based recreation of the system, starting with a blank sheet of paper.

I suppose that one response could be that regional associations and their churches are changing a great deal. They are experimenting with new forms of ministry, new ways of providing pastoral oversight, sacramental functions, and congregational involvement. However, these are generally not strategic changes; that is, change adopted to realize a stronger presence in the world. It is reactive change; that is, change adopted to ensure survival at the edge of viability. One of the most important principles for individuals and organizations to flourish in the world is simply to *change before you have to*. When organizations fail to make strategic changes, the impact may not be felt for several years; but when the door closes, it closes *very* hard.

No particular polity is assumed in these pages. The designation *regional association* is generic. Some regional associations are more hierarchical and possess more authority. Others are more voluntary. It is important that regional association leaders not dismiss the strategic implications of this book by using polity as a foil. In most systems there is more flexibility in regional polity than many leaders want to admit. In addition, there are provisions for regulatory changes in all denominational systems that may need to be considered.

The changes proposed in this book are strategic in nature. They are not focused on how to fix a specific problem. Nothing will fall apart next week if you discard them. Instead, they are focused on how to create and be ready for a better future. No parable better illustrates the necessity of making changes before you have to than the one Jesus himself gave us:

> At that time the kingdom of heaven will be like ten virgins who took
> their lamps and went out to meet the bridegroom. Five of them were
> foolish and five were wise. The foolish ones took their lamps but did

not take any oil with them. The wise, however, took oil in jars along with their lamps. The bridegroom was a long time in coming, and they all became drowsy and fell asleep. At midnight the cry rang out: "Here's the bridegroom! Come out to meet him!" Then all the virgins woke up and trimmed their lamps. The foolish ones said to the wise, "Give us some of your oil; our lamps are going out." "No," they replied, "there may not be enough for both us and you. Instead, go to those who sell oil and buy some for yourselves." But while they were on their way to buy the oil, the bridegroom arrived. The virgins who were ready went in with him to the wedding banquet. And the door was shut. (Matthew 25:1–12)

Every day that we resist necessary change closes a door of opportunity somewhere in the future. Redeveloping regional associations to be transformational is one way that the doors of the future may be opened and not shut.

Discussion Questions

For church members and leaders

1. On a scale of 1 to 10, with ten being *worried sick,* how concerned are you about the future of your congregation?

2. What would you say is your highest priority for your local church?

3. If you could ask for anything from your regional association, and be assured of receiving it, what would it be?

For regional associations

1. How have redevelopment efforts worked with local congregations in your association?

2. What are your thoughts about redeveloping your regional association to be transformational?

3. List all examples of strategic change in your regional association that have been undertaken in the last five years. Do you believe your regional association is more reactive (changing because it has to) or strategic (changing before it has to) in its approach to change?

Chapter One

GETTING THE MESSAGE CLEAR

The Really Hot, Not So Bad, Maybe OK, Half-Burning Platform

If the trumpet does not sound a clear call, who will get ready for battle? — 1 Corinthians 14:8

If we are to renew, it is because we have a vision of something worth saving or doing.[3] — John Gardner

Consultants working in the area of change management often refer to the concept of a burning platform. The term "burning platform" has been a mainstay in the business lexicon for many years. For those not familiar with its origin, the story goes something like this:

A man working on an oil platform in the North Sea was awakened suddenly one night by an explosion. Amidst the chaos, he made his way to the edge of the platform. As a plume of fire billowed behind him, he decided to jump from the burning platform even though jumping is a risky option for the following reasons:

- It was a 150-foot drop from the platform to the water.
- There is debris and burning oil on the surface of the water.
- If the jump into the 40°F water did not kill him, he would die of exposure within 15 minutes.

Luckily, the man survived the jump and was hauled aboard a rescue boat shortly thereafter. When asked why he jumped, he replied, "Better probable death than certain death." The point is that the literally "burning" platform triggered the radical change in his behavior.

In the parlance of change management, creating a burning platform means constructing a concise, compelling, evidence-based, and consistently

9

communicated rationale articulating why an organization cannot stay where it is. Its purpose is to demonstrate that the risk of maintaining the status quo is significantly higher than the risk of stepping into a future that requires considerable change. A burning platform functions as the organizational equivalent of the Biblical "hell." You don't want to be there even if it requires a leap of faith to escape it.

In seasons requiring substantial change, it is imperative that the leader sound a clear call if it is expected that people will follow into the struggle, and consequent renewal, that change will likely introduce. Unfortunately, clarity is in such short supply today that seeing through a glass darkly would be a comparative illumination.

Denominational leaders seem mired in uncertainty whether they should create a burning platform or lead a pep rally. On the one hand, leaders make statements that signal the need for significant change. In a report titled *A Wake-Up Call to the Presbyterian Church* issued in 2005, Stated Clerk Clifton Kirkpatrick wrote: "The fact that we are now into the third decade in which our annual membership numbers are showing decline is a wake-up call to the Presbyterian Church (U.S.A.)." Kirkpatrick argues that "the deepest and most profound implication is that we as a church are being called by God to prayer for repentance and renewal."[4]

Charles Fulton, director of congregational development for the Episcopal Church, responds to the 30-year numeric decline in his denomination by pondering the depths of the water: "If it's related to one event, that can be dealt with and we'll get beyond it. If it's a systemic, life cycle issue, it will be harder to turn it around, and it will require a kind of radical leadership that we don't really encourage right now. Resurrection follows death — it does not follow denial."[5]

We need to make changes! The platform is burning! We can't stay here! It is unbearably hot! But is it?

At the same time there are official voices wondering if it is so bad after all. In an article entitled "Picture Your Presbytery Here" found on the PCUSA website, Cynthia A. Woolever, Research Services Presbyterian Church (U.S.A.), writes:

> "Our presbytery suffered a net loss of members again this year. I am so discouraged." The "net loss blues" is an all too common ailment for presbytery leaders and others concerned about the future of the Presbyterian Church. But before you reach for your favorite prescription, take some time to look at the factors behind the ailment.[6]

Is the platform really burning? Or is our "crisis talking" an "all too common ailment"? Maybe it's not so bad after all!

Woolever then goes on to look at the bright side of the data, while acknowledging losses, and concludes, "The implications are clear. Continued care and nurturing of congregations of all sizes and types will yield good overall health for the presbytery in the future."[7]

It's really OK! We just need to continue what we are doing and our future is secured! What we really need is a pep rally!

I have chosen a handful of comments from a few good folks to illustrate the confused message that denominational leaders are sending to the church. It's not worth the print space to list quotes from leaders across the years indicating that all the losses are actually positive, that they indicate a separation of faithful believers from nominal members, that inflated rolls are finally being cleaned, etc. When all the pieces of the message are gathered from the four corners of Denomination Land they amount to something like "It's a really-hot-not-so-bad-maybe-OK half-burning platform." In contrast to denominational leaders, church members are remarkably unconfused about the state of things. As we shall see, their priorities and concerns are clear and consistent.

Now the reader may be thinking something like this: "Of course there are different perspectives on the need for change. It is natural and appropriate for there to be free and open debate about these issues at the highest levels of the church." My response is simply this: I do not know of a single effective organization today in either the profit or nonprofit realm that is still debating the need for substantial change in the way they go about accomplishing their mission. If the denominational leadership wants to continue to debate the need for change, it will have to accept the consequential decline in the system as a whole. There will be bright spots scattered about, but these will be led by persons who have figured out effective strategies on their own, often in reaction to the inertia of the system. Church leaders cannot expect folks to charge into the chaos of system change if they continue to sound such an ambiguous call.

Good communication skills are a core leadership requirement. In situations that call for significant change, clear communication makes or breaks the process. The first step in creating a transformational regional association is to realize that the primary target audience for the case for change is not members of churches but key players in the systems, including pastors, regional association leaders, and higher-level denominational leaders.

Strategically, members of congregations are keenly aware of the need to grow and revitalize their churches. Having surveyed tens of thousands of church members I can say without equivocation that the number one priority for members is to invest additional energy into reaching new members and the number two priority is making necessary changes to attract families with children and youth. This is true in 95 percent of the churches surveyed and has not changed significantly in 20 years of data gathering. Church members have sparkling clarity on this issue.

In addition, when church leaders are asked to indicate priorities for their regional association, their number one priority is equipping pastors and other church leaders with strategies that will help them grow and revitalize their churches. No "wake-up" call is needed; I would urge that we cease upon that particular bugle. Church members are awake! They don't need more "pow"! They need more "how"! But where are the persons who will allocate the time, money, expertise, and spiritual juice to provide the "how"? This, it seems to me, falls squarely in the lap of regional association leaders and is the opportunity that calls for the redevelopment of those associations.

There is a question here that screams for an answer: What does it mean that we have denominational leaders sounding wake-up calls for the church to *become* more concerned about reaching new persons, when all the research indicates that the number one concern for members *is* reaching new persons? It suggests to me that we have denominational systems in the middle that are unaligned with that goal and that these systems are robust in their resistance to change.

Clifton Kirkpatrick listed six imperatives for one Presbyterian Church to "rise again":

1. We need to realize that our most important evangelistic outreach begins at home.

2. We need to follow the wisdom of the *Book of Order* concerning inactive members.

3. Jesus was quite clear in the Great Commission that we as followers of Christ are called to make disciples of all nations by baptizing them (Matthew 28:19).

4. We need to learn from our growing churches and imitate them!

5. If we are going to be a growing church, we must be a multicultural church.

6. We need to start more new churches.[8]

Kirkpatrick has provided a respectable list of strategic initiatives that few members would argue with. What is missing is the necessary revamping of denominational systems to provide the focus, resources, and expertise to make this happen, specifically at the level of the regional association. I would argue that Charles Fulton has it right: we *are* dealing with a "systemic, life cycle issue, [that] will be harder to turn it around, and it will require a kind of radical leadership that we don't really encourage right now."

So, for the sake of the blessed clarity which I espouse, let me sharpen the lines. If systematic change is going to occur, not just for a few churches, but for the majority, the locus of that change will need to be the regional association. Leading that change will require the clearest, most compelling, and most consistently communicated rationale of all. Without a change in this middle body, we will simply become noisy gongs sounding wake-up calls to rooms vacated by people who wanted to learn something beyond what an alarm could teach them.

Discussion Questions

For church members and leaders

1. What is your vision for what your church will look like in three to five years?

2. Do you know how to get there? What do you think your church needs to learn how to do?

3. What is the basic message you are hearing from your regional association regarding what you need to be doing? How clear is that message?

For regional associations

1. How would you respond to Clifton Kirkpatrick's wake-up call? Is it strong enough? Too strong?

2. What do you think about Charles Fulton's analysis? Are we dealing with a systemic, life-cycle issue that calls for a radical kind of new leadership?

3. How clear is your regional association about the need for change?

Chapter Two

BEYOND TWO-SKUNK SOLUTIONS

*Only through such transformation or contextual
shift can an individual, a work unit, an organization,
or a society break the self-limiting barriers imposed
by the old frame of reference and open up to the
possibility of renewal.*[9]   — John Williamson

There once was a woman who lived in a house by the woods. One evening she absentmindedly left the outside basement door open. When she went down the basement stairs to do laundry the next morning, she was startled by a skunk that had entered during the night.

Dismayed by the prospect of being sprayed by a skunk but unsure what to do, she called the local department of natural resources and asked a ranger for advice. "It is really quite simple," the ranger said. "Leave the door open again tonight, but before you go to bed place a trail of bread crumbs from the basement door to the woods."

"That's not so hard," she thought to herself, and went about her other work. That evening, before she went to bed, she placed a trail of bread crumbs from the basement door to the woods, just like the ranger had instructed her.

The next morning the phone rang in the ranger station. "Sir, I did what you said. Now I have two skunks in my basement."

The story illustrates what I refer to as two-skunk solutions. Two-skunk solutions inadvertently create problems that are simply replications of existing ones. Denominational efforts in the 1980s and 1990s to prop up marginally sized congregations with financial supplements simply resulted in more marginally sized congregations. Fostering dependency is generally a two-skunk solution that feels like help but simply generates more dependency.

When we do not think deeply enough about a problem, we create two-skunk solutions. The chronic use of credit cards to cover a consistent

14

shortfall in income is a solution that simply creates a second, similar problem. As Einstein put it, "In order to solve a problem, you have to think in a different way than what created the problem in the first place."

Even the best of solutions creates new problems. But the goal of solving problems is not to eliminate problems but to create *higher* problems. Jesus solves the hunger problem of the five thousand by feeding them. But this solution simply introduces a higher-level problem: how do you nourish a sense of meaning and purpose in your life? Jesus shatters the illusion of a life without problems; the goal of any endeavor is not to eliminate problems but to create and then engage higher-level issues.

The effort to redevelop a regional association is not aimed at eliminating problems; it is aimed at engaging higher-level problems. Denominations are failing to make the changes that are necessary to cultivate vital, healthy congregations. Instead, they are engaging in relatively superficial solutions that not only fail as solutions but replicate existing problems. Just as we confess our small sins to avoid confessing more serious ones, denominations are engaging low-level issues in order to avoid dealing with more substantive ones. Endless reorganizations, "new" mission statements, salvation by language all feel like change, but they are usually little more than a fresh coat of paint.

There are many noble reasons for focusing on higher-level problems: mission effectiveness, creation of meaning, spiritual growth, rich team experiences. But my favorite is simply that they are more fun to solve even at their most difficult. That, I believe, is why Jesus told parables. A parable is a kind of puzzle that invites the reader to engage in a quest for solution. Once the puzzle is solved, the reader is taken to another level; the reader "owns" the solution at a higher level than if the answer had simply been given away.

So let me say up front to clergy, board members, church members, and regional association leaders: my goal is not to make your life easier by eliminating problems; my goal is to make your life richer by challenging you to engage the higher problems that are truly worthy of your soul's endeavor. Paradoxically, what we avoid only makes life harder.

The Challenge of Church Leadership

This book is sympathetic to the challenge of church leadership. How hard is it to lead in the church today? Business consultant Peter Drucker suggested that the three toughest management jobs in the United States are university president, hospital CEO, and senior pastor of a large church. From research conducted with thousands of members in hundreds of churches, on average only

16

Table 2.1. The Level of Satisfaction of Communities with
Their Public Libraries Compared to Church Members with Their Churches

Organization Type	Clearly Negative	On the Fence	Clearly Positive
Typical Public Library	2%	11%	87%
Typical Church	6%	39%	55%

Sources: *Church Assessment Tool* © and *Patron Assessment Tool* ©

55 percent of members are clearly satisfied overall with what is happening in their church. By way of comparison, over 85 percent of members in an average community are clearly satisfied with their local public library (see Table 2.1).

The problem we are facing is not simply a numeric decline, but churches where members indicate such poor quality of community life that it is difficult to invite new people into them. From the standpoint of the satisfaction with their experience, it is easier to make the case for folks to get a library card than to join the typical denominational church in their community! With some notable exceptions, few of us are exclaiming with the Apostle Paul, "my brothers, you whom I love and long for, my joy and crown" (Philippians 4:1). No wonder the career mortality rates of new seminary graduates is so high. In a landmark study of seminaries and their graduates (Appendix C), Carolyn Weese found that only one in five seminary graduates continued in ministry five years after graduation.

What clergy are experiencing at the helm of leadership, church board members are experiencing on deck. The seas are rough for both; the same wind and spray buffets them all. At any particular board meeting important decisions are made, most of which would receive the support of a majority of the congregation, but none is likely to be energetically and enthusiastically embraced. Burn-out at least implies a fire, but rust-out (burn-out at room temperature) is the more likely destination for the average board member.

Transformational Churches

The reader might be tempted to heave a sigh of resignation at this point: "That's just the way it is with churches! We're *supposed* to be struggling! Jesus called us to pick up our crosses and follow him! That pretty much means that if something is making our life as a church unsatisfying, it is our cross to bear. These low levels of energy and satisfaction are simply a reflection of a life of discipleship!"

This response might be more convincing were it not for the fact that what is true for the *average* church is not true for *every* church. The problem with the word "average" is that it obscures what is happening at the edges. As is commonly noted in statistics classes, if a man has one foot in a bucket of ice water and one foot in a bucket of boiling water, on average he should be comfortable!

As I said above, a few churches are notable exceptions. I call them transformational churches. In transformational churches, over 80 percent of members are clearly satisfied with what is happening. The data shows that this cannot be simply dismissed as the delusions of a self-satisfied, organizational narcissism. These churches have members who are open and hospitable to one another, who are broadly involved in the decision-making of the church, who experience inspiring and transformational worship, who are engaged in significant ministry opportunities in the church and to the world, and who overwhelmingly affirm that the church has given new meaning to their lives. Leadership in these churches, for both clergy and board members, is a radically different experience.

With the right changes, I believe the majority of churches in America could experience what these transformational churches have discovered. They need help in knowing what those right changes are. And they need encouragement to change. Which organization is best positioned to help clergy and church boards develop themselves into transformational churches?

I believe it is the presbytery, diocese, synod, district, or conference of which they are a part. Their names vary by polity. To coin a generic term, I have called them regional associations. A good case can be made that these regional associations are the best choice for developing transformational churches. They understand the local environment. They have a grasp of the particular polity. Travel to local congregations is not burdensome. They can do on-site training, mentoring, and facilitation without it costing an arm and a leg and a gold filling.

The Problem of Low Morale in Regional Associations

How are things going for regional associations? Not so well. Our research suggests that only a third of those served by a regional association is typically satisfied with what is happening. Serving as a leader in a local church with only 55 percent of membership clearly satisfied is tough enough.

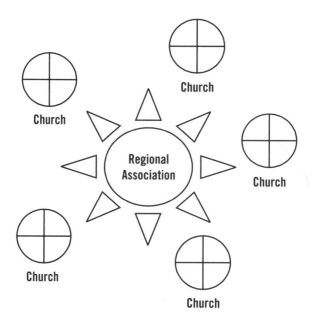

Figure 2.2. Regional Association

Regional Associations have many different names and structures. Many are traditional, denominational structures. Others are forming around cyber-networks as local church leaders look to larger churches for resources and support. Some multi-site churches are *de facto* regional associations with centralized governance.

When only a third of the folks you are leading feel positive, movement is almost impossible. Contrast this with the level of satisfaction of persons served in a pediatric emergency department where roughly 85 percent of respondents are clearly satisfied. Compared to the members of a presbytery, for example, we are almost three times more likely to find a satisfied person walking out of an emergency department and they have just waited, on average, three hours for their sick or injured child to see a doctor.

Some respond to this type of data on member satisfaction with the assertion that members of churches and regional associations simply have higher standards than other organizations and that satisfaction is not a good measure of their morale. Other measures clearly indicate that this is not the case. In both churches and regional associations, about one in five respondents

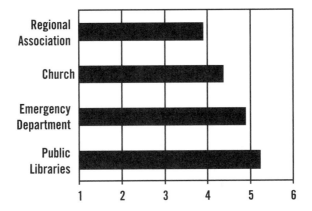

Figure 2.3. Average Overall Satisfaction Scores
for Four Different Organizations

Scale: 1=Strongly disagree; 2=Disagree; 3=Tend to disagree; 4=Tend to agree; 5=Agree; 6=Strongly agree

Sources: *Church Assessment Tool* ©, *Patron Assessment Tool* ©, *Regional Association Assessment Tool* ©

feels that the church is just going through the motions with another two in five on the fence regarding the question.

For 40 years, the argument has been made that the number of persons in a church is not that important. It is not the *quantity* of people in a church that matters, but the *quality* of their experience. That artificial distinction does not hold up. It is difficult to make the case that we should invite new members into a church where many of them will become like the rest of us, unable to say that we are doing anything meaningful or exciting. And it is equally difficult to make the case that new clergy should enter a regional association where a large percentage of them will end up feeling, to one degree or another, that they are just going through the motions.

My message is simple: By avoiding the high-level problems that need to be addressed, we are perpetuating the kind of low morale that makes life difficult.

Making Life Richer

You may be a member of the clergy: pastor, rector, minister, priest, deacon, elder, vicar, or leader by another name.

You may be a member of your local church's governance: board, vestry, session, consistory, committee, commission, or leader by another name.

You may be the leader of a regional association: bishop, executive presbyter, district superintendent, conference president, executive pastor, or regional leader by another name.

You may simply be a member of a regional association or a local church.

My purpose is to make your shared life a richer experience. "But," you say, "we have particular issues in our denomination that require our life to be difficult. We must address those specific issues before our life can be easier." I do not believe that is true. Simply put, I believe that if the prominent issues in any particular denomination were to magically go away, our levels of satisfaction would not significantly change. In fact, I believe that our systems would find new issues to support our unhappiness.

Are we not called to suffer for the Gospel? Is there not a price for discipleship? Of course we are and of course there is. But Scripture teaches us that there is no virtue in suffering for what lies within our power to correct. "But how is it to your credit if you receive a beating for doing wrong and endure it?" (1 Peter 2:20). Many people are simply unwilling to pay the personal price that denominational churches are exacting, a price not for the sake of the Gospel, but for the sake of organizations that are unwilling to learn. I fear, in the words of Jesus, that we are loading people down with burdens they can hardly carry.

The refusal of local church members and their leaders to make the sacrifice is often chalked up to an unwillingness of those in our culture to break out of their narcissistic mind-set. After several years of directing two international nonprofits, I do not find this assertion to be consistent with my experience. I find that people are generally desperate for opportunities to contribute to the world, to express their generosity, and to find meaning through service. I have observed hundreds of people every year spend over a thousand dollars of their own money, give up a week of their paid vacation, endure inoculations, heat, humidity, mosquitoes, scorpions, and long hours of manual labor in the hot, tropical sun in order to provide a home for children with HIV. And I have watched persons who cannot make such a trip offer up hundreds of thousands of dollars for the cause.

What people seem to be saying to denominational systems is this: we are willing to sacrifice to make a better world in the name of Jesus; we are not willing to sacrifice for ecclesiastical systems that absorb our time, our energy, and our money and then seek to justify it as the price of being a "community."

While most of my data and experience has been collected from the Presbyterian and Episcopal traditions, the problems that we must address cross the theological and polity spectrum. Recently, I was meeting with a consultant from the Assembly of God church. He asked what I was writing. I outlined for him the problems of culture, perception, tools, and sin in the local church–regional association relationship. When I finished, he smiled and said, "You have just described the Assembly of God Church."

"The girl that can't dance says the band can't play." Because we are avoiding the critical issues that could reshape our regional associations into agents of congregational renewal, we end up blaming the band — the issue of the day, the times in which we live, one another. Switching to another metaphor, when the body is weak, almost any virus can make us sick.

The title of this book, *The Fly in the Ointment*, is meant to reflect an optimistic perspective. An ointment is a remedy. A fly in the ointment is something that spoils a treatment which could have been successful. Successful, they can be. But the fly that obviates the potential help and healing these bodies might offer to local churches is an aversion to well-known and fundamental principles of organizational health. Organizationally, we insist on junk food and then pray for a miracle at the hour of our demise.

Today denominational leaders of all stripes cite increasingly dire statistics and sound "wake-up calls." Unfortunately, these often amount to panicked pleas for members to work harder at what doesn't work. They did not work in 1977, ten years into the decline, and they did not work in 2007, 40 years into the decline. What is required is a deep, systemic change in the bodies that are called to support congregations for their mission in the world: transformational regional associations.

Discussion Questions

For church members and leaders

1. If you grew up in a church, what was the regional association called that your church was connected to (e.g., diocese, presbytery, conference, synod, etc.)?

2. If your regional association were to suddenly disappear today, what would be the effect on your local congregation?

3. This chapter suggests that regional associations may be avoiding the kinds of changes that would help strengthen local congregations. What are your thoughts on this?

4. Tell about a time that your regional association helped your church in a significant way.

For regional associations

1. This chapter indicates that only about a third of leaders in a regional association are typically satisfied with what that association is doing. Do you think that is about the same in your regional association?

2. Is there a controversy currently brewing in your regional association? If that were to suddenly be resolved, do you think that most people would be satisfied with your regional association? Why or why not?

3. This chapter indicates that only about 55 percent of persons in a typical church are generally satisfied overall and that on average, people are less satisfied with their church than they are with their public library or an emergency room visit. Why do you think this is?

Chapter Three

SMART LOVE IN A "FOR DUMMIES" CULTURE

All things by immortal power
Near or far
Hiddenly
To each other linked are
That thou cans't not stir a flower
Without troubling a star.[10]
— Francis Thompson

I once asked an executive vice president who was
responsible for the future development of a very large
corporation, "What is the thing you worry about
most on your job?" His answer was startling. "I
worry most about what my people don't know that
they don't know. What they know that they don't
know, they are able to work on and find the answers
to. But they can't do that if they don't know that
they don't know."[11] — Stanley M. Davis

For many people the longest line in the world is the distance between God and a book on church organization. But in the Appalachian idiom of my father, I believe it is a mere hop, skip, and a jump. I have watched poor processes and structure absolutely wreck the best efforts of good folks with the deepest spiritual commitments and the highest aspirations for the Body of Christ.

The spiritual gift of administration is often the stepchild of the church, but what the gift of preaching may build and what the gift of healing may remedy can be largely undone by slipshod administration. People mentally equate administration with bureaucracy; they imagine inaccessible people sitting behind desks buried in policies and procedures. In reality, the gift of administration provides the organizational blueprint for the Body of Christ, specifies how all the parts are arranged, and serves as the ligaments that hold all the parts together so that the Body can function without fear that a hand might fall off when the arm is called into action.

Others appear to believe that matters of organizational strategy and function are intuitive. They require no training, and have no body of content that must be mastered. It is interesting that the same people who would argue that theological training is required for responsible church leadership often believe that a group of well-intentioned leaders should be able to brainstorm their way to effectiveness when it comes to subjects like marketing, strategy, and organizational design.

The gift of administration gives members of the Body the practical tools to do the work of ministry. I grew up in a family that was relatively poor from a financial standpoint. When I was a boy I would watch my father work on our less than reliable car using only screwdrivers, a pair of vise grips, and a crescent wrench. He found it to be an extremely frustrating experience. On several occasions, I remember him pausing as if he needed a break from exasperation, looking up at me and saying, "If I just had the right tools, I could do anything." For the craftsman of any trade, tools are not a cold, boring addition to the "real" work. They are a gift of grace. When my father could finally afford a socket set, it was a kind of sacramental expression of God's love for him. That is how I view the offering of this book.

In this chapter, I will begin to ground this book theologically by exploring the implications of the Trinity as a source of guidance for the work. I want to look at the danger of specialism and advocate for the riches that lie in affirming the connection of all creation in the unity of God. Then I will look at how organizations and organisms grow, develop—and stagnate. Finally, I will argue that the critical issue for churches today is developing a "smart love" and that transformational regional association leaders (e.g., bishops, presbyters, executives, etc.) are in the best position to support that process.

The Trinity as an Antidote to Specialism

The concept of the Trinity may be one of the greatest gifts that Christianity has given to the world. I have to admit that early in my Christian life I found the Trinity to be ethereal, abstract, and intellectually embarrassing. It struck me as a kind of theological fruitcake of disparate ideas chunked together and baked in a political oven at high temperature. Now I find myself an enthusiastic convert.

My conversion was triggered by an epiphany that the Trinity not only tells us something important about God, but gives us insight into the nature of reality itself. A look into a night sky spangled with stars offers more than an emotional sigh that something greater than ourselves must exist. The heavens can "declare the glory of God" precisely because the universe speaks from the reality that God has stamped into its very structure. Like the Trinity, the cosmos is an essential unity with multiple expressions, intimately connected and fundamentally one. Each part of the universe is in service to every other part and each can teach and learn from every other. The same is true of human relationships and the organizations they create.

This understanding flies in the face of a modern tendency toward *specialism* which I define as "an exclusive devotion to a particular and restricted part or branch of knowledge, art, or science." Specialism goes beyond specialization. *Specialization* refers to "being designed, trained, or fitted for a particular purpose"; *specialism,* by being an 'ism,' cuts the cord that connects all things and sets them adrift as non-communicating islands. In the church, a specialistic orientation fosters the attitude that we have little to learn from other types of organizations, sacred or secular.

Organizations of all kinds, profit and nonprofit, are passing through a significant period of metamorphosis. We often romanticize the transformation of a caterpillar into a butterfly, but the process within the cocoon is chemically violent. Having watched numerous organizations make changes essential to their future success, I can attest that it is not an easy road. For those in the church, we must stop feeling sorry for ourselves and get on with the same kind of transformational work. We are not alone on the journey. But when we succumb to specialism, we break the link that connects organization to organization and consequently abort the learning process.

I can make this concrete by relating an exchange that I observed several years ago between a local church leader and a leader within the church's denominational system. The particular issue in play concerned an imminent pastoral transition. The denominational leader had indicated it would take an 18- to 24-month search process to call the next pastor. The lay leader responded by saying, "I hire college presidents for a living. If I said to my clients what you have just said to us, I would be fired." The answer of the denominational leader was reflexive: "The church is different." That response placed a definite period at the end of the discussion. This is specialism at its sharpest expression.

I have observed a repeat of this specialistic conversation around other issues with some distressing regularity. Though unintended, the result is the effective neutralization of many of the gifts that lay people bring to the table from their experiences in the world, the world filled and held together by Christ (Colossians 1:17). I have sat with relatively silent church leaders at table after table only to discover in later, more private conversations that they have gifts that could help the Body of Christ, but no way to offer them. Dr. Linda Karlovec, friend and organizational psychologist, calls this a learned helplessness. I call it a consequence of specialism.

While the church *is* different, the Trinity suggests that the church also shares a fundamental unity with the rest of the cosmos and with other organizations that have formed in this spiraled arm of what we call the Milky Way galaxy. What is exciting about this understanding is the discovery that God has something to teach us everywhere we turn. So let's start with the alphabet.

The Ubiquitous S-Curve

One of my favorite characters of the English alphabet is the letter "S." As a single, smooth stroke it possesses an elegance that I find beguiling. But there is another reason for my affection toward this shape. The "S-curve" represents the developmental path of many diverse organisms and organizations that we experience every day.

Figure 3.1 is a horizontally stretched version of the S-curve. It is deceptively simple. It basically represents how organisms and organizations grow and develop over time. It applies to the physical growth of human beings and flatworms,[12] bacteria in a Petri dish and the population of cities, the sale of VHS machines and the improvement of morale in an organization. It also applies to churches.

There are basically three phases to the growth/development process. In the Organizing Phase, the entity is investing energy in self-organization; growth is slow. For a church, this may involve recruiting and training leaders, building a facility, and creating a structure. In the Replication Phase the entity can turn its attention to a reproductive function in which it is repeating what it learned in the Organizing Phase with a larger and larger "body." Growth is rapid during this phase. However, growth comes at the cost of consuming an increasing number of *critical resources*. Eventually the entity depletes one or more critical resources, which slows down or stops its growth. It has entered the Stable Phase. For example, churches may run out

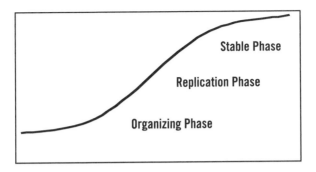

Figure 3.1. How Organisms Grow and Develop
The vertical axis represents growth/development; the horizontal axis represents time.

of parking, entry-point fellowship opportunities, staff leadership, or sanctuary seating space. Here change creeps to a near standstill. Relatively small improvements take a long time to realize. Churches either stop growing altogether, or, if the environment shifts, begin to decline.

When an organism enters the Stable Phase, it faces a choice. It must either choose to stop growing or find a way to replenish the critical resource that has been exhausted in the growth process; e.g., expand the facility, purchase property for more parking, or add staff. In the infant church of the New Testament, the critical resource of administrative oversight was depleted, resulting in a lack of care for Greek-speaking widows. This resource was replenished by creating the diaconal ministry led by the soon-to-be-martyred and courageous Stephen. With his appointment, the church could then reenter the Replication Phase and continue to grow.

Since most denominational churches are plateaued or have been declining now for about 40 years, we can assume that there is a system-wide depletion of one or more critical resources that has halted replication. What is it?

In Search of the Missing Resource

There are several possibilities for what the missing resource might be:

- Church members lack the desire for church growth.
- Church leaders lack the desire for church growth.
- Church members have lost their faith and are spiritually depleted.
- Church members are "unfriendly."

Table 3.2. Where Members Want Additional Energy Invested
in the Future: Top Five Priorities

Rank	Goal
First Priority	Develop and implement a comprehensive strategy to reach new people and incorporate them into the life of the church.
Second Priority	Make necessary changes to attract families with children and youth to our church.
Third Priority	Move decisively to provide high-quality education for every age and stage of life.
Fourth Priority	Develop ministries that work toward healing those broken by life circumstances.
Fifth Priority	Develop the spiritual generosity of the people to financially support the ministry of the church.

Source: *Church Assessment Tool* ©

- Churches do not have enough facility space.
- Churches lack the know-how to grow vital, healthy churches.

I will now take a look at each of these options.

Has the desire for growth declined among congregations? The evidence clearly indicates that the answer is "no." Congregational surveys of thousands of congregants indicate that the number one priority is "develop and implement a comprehensive strategy to reach new people and incorporate them into the life of the church." Two-thirds of respondents indicate this should receive a high level or a substantial level of additional energy in the coming year.

Table 3.2 lists the top five priorities of members for the investment of additional energy in the future. The first two priorities express a direct interest in the growth of the church and the third is often intended as a necessary prerequisite to attracting families.

Has the desire for growth declined for leaders of congregations? Again, the evidence indicates that the answer is "no." Survey responses from over 1,000 leaders indicate that the number one priority is "equip pastors and

Table 3.3. Where Pastors Want to Invest Additional Energy
in the Future: Top Five Priorities

Rank	Goal
First Priority	Deepen a congregation's sense of connection to God and one another through stronger worship services.
Second Priority	Provide opportunities for Christian education and spiritual formation in a church for every age and stage of life.
Third Priority	Make necessary changes in a church to attract families with children and youth.
Fourth Priority	Develop and implement a comprehensive strategy to reach new people and incorporate them into the life of a church.
Fifth Priority	Create more opportunities for people to form meaningful relationships (for example, small groups, nurtured friendships, shared meals, etc.).

Source: *Passion Effectiveness Tool* ©

other leaders in congregations with strategies that enable them to reach new members and help them become growing, vital disciples." Nearly nine out of ten leaders indicated they would be more satisfied with their regional association if it were able to help them do this. Supporting that finding are the results of a survey of pastors designed to better understand where they would like to invest additional energy in the future. These results are found in Table 3.3.

Are churches filled with members who have totally depleted their faith? No, again. Roughly nine out of ten agree to one degree or another that their spirituality is really the basis of their entire lives. Members score themselves higher on spiritual vitality than any other questions posed to them in a congregational survey. The mean scores on these questions can be found in Figure 3.4.

Have we depleted our friendliness? Apparently not. Over 90 percent of the members in a typical church believe they are a friendly lot.

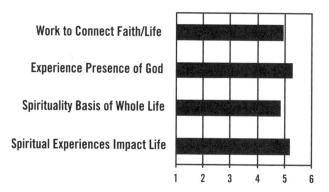

Figure 3.4. Average Scores for Spiritual Vitality

Scale: 1=Strongly disagree; 2=Disagree; 3=Tend to disagree; 4=Tend to agree; 5=Agree; 6=Strongly agree

Source: *Church Assessment Tool ©*

Have churches run out of facility space? A final "no." Denominational churches exhibit row after row of empty pews on a typical Sunday morning. The space may be in critical need of renovation and upgrading, but the average space per member is likely at an all-time high. On the whole, we have plenty of facility space.

Knowledge and Insight

Summing up, we have churches with members who want the church to grow, led by leaders who want the church to grow with room in their facilities for new people. So what is the critical resource that has been depleted? I would argue there are two: knowledge and insight. Knowledge I define as reliable information on how to develop a healthy, vital church. Depth of insight I define as the capacity to connect knowledge to context; that is, how to effectively integrate knowledge into the life of a particular body in a particular community. Insight, as one person put it, is not new information; it is rearranging the information you already have so that it works for you.

People today are simultaneously experiencing information overload and insight deprivation. They have more information (knowledge) bombarding them than they can assimilate. At the same time they are bewildered at how to integrate what they are learning into their daily lives (insight). This has created the "for dummies" culture. The paradigmatic symbol of the dummy culture is the video player that comes complete with an operator's manual but offers the equivalent experience of a tablet of Egyptian hieroglyphics in one hand and a Rosetta stone in the other (Styrofoam versions!). People in the dummy culture are not offended by the implication that they are clueless about a subject; they find it mildly affirming that they are not alone. Bookshelves abound with "*anything* for dummies" and "*everything* for idiots" titles.

Collectively, churches often believe that they should be magically exempt from the need to develop their store of knowledge and insight about how to develop healthy, vital congregations. They put all their eggs in the baskets of good intentions (love) and faith. We would never think about going to an unschooled surgeon armed only with a diploma of good intentions or a pharmacist with a degree in hotel management because he is such a nice guy. Yet we have trouble admitting it when we don't know what we are doing. This is simply another symptom of our failure to identify folks in the Body of Christ who have the administrative gifts and practical experience that can help the body upbuild itself in love.

Paul did not have that problem. In the book of Philippians, Paul tells the churches that he "prays that their love might abound in knowledge and depth of insight" (Phil. 1:6). Puny knowledge; puny love! Love cannot abound, its full fruit cannot be realized in the world if it is not equipped with knowledge and insight, information and integration. In other words, knowledge and insight, information and integration, are critical resources for the health of the Body of Christ. Paul is arguing for a *smart love*. If love has not been formed in the soul by the working of the Holy Spirit, no amount of knowledge or insight will serve as an adequate substitute. But when love is not equipped, not "smart," the Body stops building itself up in love (replicating) and often begins to decline.

When We Don't Know What We Don't Know

When knowledge and insight are depleted, we are usually unaware of the magnitude of the deficit. To put it another way, *we do not know what we do not know*. This is nearly tautological. Ignorance can only be evaluated in retrospect from the perspective of knowledge. I cannot tell you what I do not know about being a stock broker until I am actually trained as a stock broker and then contrast myself before and now.

When an entire organization is depleted of knowledge and insight, brainstorming is ineffective. As one consultant put it, brainstorming in a church where people are admittedly lost as to what to do merely results in a pooling of ignorance. While brainstorming can optimize the available knowledge in a group of people, it does not make up for a lack of understanding when an important body of content is missing. We would never think of brainstorming how to do heart surgery!

Beyond learning all about a subject myself, there is one way to know what I don't know: through a trusted guide. My daughter is a lawyer. I cannot tell you how much I do not know about the law. But she can. If I am teachable and if I trust her, I can arrive at a good estimate of what I don't know. These attitudes — teachability and trust — expressed in relationship to God are the beginning of wisdom. In the Body of Christ, they are the beginning of developing a vital church. The bottom line is that a leader cannot lead beyond his or her level of knowledge and understanding.

If knowledge and insight are the depleted resources that have arrested the development of congregations, their recovery will have two requirements: a teachable spirit on the part of the members of congregations and their members, and trust in a mentor or teacher who has gone before them and who knows what they do not know.

Transformational regional associations will need to provide the kinds of resources, coaching, and expertise that will bridge this gap in knowledge and insight. This is what church leaders are asking for! Local church leaders will need to develop teachable spirits and renew their trust that these associations have something to offer them. This task is not trivial. If taken seriously, the redevelopment of a regional association will impact every aspect of its organization beginning with the kind of leadership necessary for its success. That is the topic addressed in the next chapter.

Discussion Questions

For church members and leaders

1. Tell about an important lesson you learned about life outside of your church experience.

2. Did you ever feel that you had something important that you would like to give to the church, but you didn't know how to give it? Can you talk about that?

3. What are some of the different opinions you hear regarding why denominational churches have stopped growing or are in decline? How confident do you feel that any of those opinions are correct?

4. How much training have your members received on what it takes to grow a healthy, vital church in today's world? Do you think it is enough?

5. Do you believe that the members of the church are teachable? Are you teachable?

6. What would it take for you to trust your regional association leader (bishop, presbyter, executive, etc.) to provide you with the knowledge and insight to help your church become stronger?

For regional associations

1. What would you say is the level of expertise that your regional association offers congregations in developing health and vitality?

2. What would you say is the level of trust among your member churches that your regional association has something to offer them?

3. What would it take to develop the teachability and trust referred to in this chapter?

Chapter Four

ORGANIZATIONAL LEVEL DYNAMICS

*All management theories are correct and can help you
when applied in the right context. All management
theories are wrong and can hinder you in the wrong
context. It all depends on where you are.*

— anonymous

*There is a time for everything, and a season for every
activity under heaven.* — Ecclesiastes 3:1

The most important and radical tasks in redeveloping regional associations
into transformational bodies are recruiting, developing, and retaining the
right leadership. The right leadership will be capable of functioning in a
way that is suitable for the *size* of the organization and appropriate to
their leadership *level* within the organization. This chapter makes the case
that regional associations are not able to provide what local churches need
because they do not understand organizational level dynamics and are functioning with values, skills, and time management that are inappropriate to
the regional level.

As we trace the development of the disciples we see them first struggling
with the function of managing themselves under the teaching of Jesus. After
the resurrection, they assume the function of managing ministries to others.
As the church grows, they begin to hear complaints that the widows of
Hellenistic Jews are being neglected in the daily distribution of food. As
a result, they must shift their function once again. They appoint others to
manage the daily distribution of food and become managers of managers.
Finally, it is necessary for some to manage a regional association of churches;
that is, to become bishops or presbyters.

There are four basic levels of management in this progression, shown in
Figure 4.1. These levels are represented against the backdrop of a pyramid in
order to represent the decreasing numbers of persons required at each level.

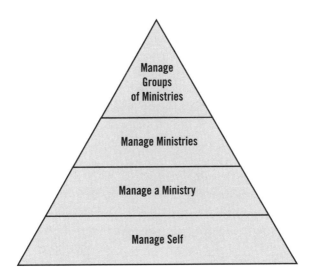

Figure 4.1. The Four Levels of Management

Level 1: Everyone must manage himself or herself. Therefore, that level is at the base and is the broadest. Level 2: Many will manage ministries; that is, groups of persons committed to a particular area of service such as teaching or overseeing finances. Level 3: Fewer will manage ministries by serving at the helm of the church either as ordained clergy or lay leader. Level 4: Fewer still will serve in the level of managing groups of churches. This is the level of the regional association leader.

While the same person may make his way up through the organization by serving in each of these roles, the function at each level is distinct. The capacity to function well at one particular level does not guarantee success at other levels. Many school teachers become school principals. But success as a teacher does not guarantee success as a principal. Leadership is not a generic set of qualities immediately transferable from one level to another.

Each level requires different skills, values, and time commitments. The leader who cannot make the shift may find himself or herself failing at one organizational level after fabulous success at a previous level. This is not only bewildering to the individual; it impedes the organization in fulfilling its mission.

The best pool of potential leaders will be those who have been successful at previous levels within the organization. A person who regularly erupts in \

anger and verbal abuse cannot manage himself and should not be managing others until he learns to do so. This is the notion behind the Biblical requirement that a leader be able to manage his own household; if he cannot manage his own household he has no business managing the household of God (1 Timothy 3:5). On the other hand, the very attributes that make a person successful at one level may defeat him at another if he does not let them go. A star athlete will fail at coaching if he keeps running onto the field and making tackles, no matter how fantastic the tackles. People who are excellent pastors in their local churches may not be suited as leaders in transformational regional associations.

Organizational level dynamics define the different values, skills, and time commitments required at different points within the organization. By and large, clergy already have a way of understanding this concept. As I travel across the country, I find that most clergy have become fluent in the language of **organizational size dynamics.** They understand that a family-size church is distinct from a resource-size church and therefore requires a different leadership style. This is true even if the core mission of both churches is the same. The increased sophistication required by this understanding represents a significant step forward in the church culture; it signals that church leaders are able to make a distinction between mission and tactics, between *what* church leaders feel called to accomplish and *how* they will go about doing it. Potentially, this frees leaders to learn from other organizational disciplines and to resist the temptation to sacralize a particular organizational design.

Potentially! While it is clear that many clergy understand *size dynamics* at the congregational level, the implications of that understanding have not expanded to include *level dynamics.* Clergy are able to talk about leadership style and organizational structure in a congregation as a variable that relates to size. But suddenly, at the level of regional associations, the same clergy sacralize a particular style and function as if it were solely a theological or ecclesiastical issue. To function as a leader in a regional association in the same way that one would function as leader in a local church is like trying to be the pastor of an 8,000-member church in the same way one would be the pastor of a 100-member church.

The role of a regional association leader is significantly different from that of parish leadership whether that is embodied in a single office such as a bishop or a superintendent or formed corporately in a presbytery or conference. This is largely a matter of location within the organizational structure — that is, level dynamics. The problem is that when parish leaders cross the threshold into the function of a regional association they often are not clear enough about the shift that is taking place to consciously say to themselves, "I am no longer functioning at the level of parish leader. I must now take on a different set of leadership values, call forth a different set of skills, and allocate my time according to a different set of priorities." As a result they may carry into that leadership role a set of values, skills, and time commitments that are debilitating at the regional level.[13]

Can leaders be trained to make this shift in thinking? I believe the answer is "yes." Leaders have already learned to make this kind of shift as they move from one size church to another. There is every reason to believe that leaders could make this shift from the local parish to their regional association if they were given the concepts, language, and training appropriate to that level.

Leadership Values for Regional Association Leaders

So what must leaders in transformational regional associations value above all else? *The effectiveness of the churches they oversee*. I don't want to get into a verbal contest at this point over what makes a church effective. That will come later. I merely want to argue that, whatever the criteria, a regional association leader must value seeing member churches flourish.

I am using the word *value* as a verb rather than a noun. I am not referring to a list of qualities generated by a brainstorming session and posted on a flip chart. I am speaking of a personal attribute, a description of how a person is emotionally and intellectually wired. To value something is to acquire energy from it to such an extent that you are motivated to seek more of it. What you do for a living provides you with a monetary paycheck. What you value provides you with an emotional paycheck. In the best of all worlds, these are the same.

There are four basic values that must shape your work as a regional association leader:

1. You must value indirect success; that is, success through others.
2. You must value strategic engagement with your member congregations.
3. You must value the development of a pool of high-quality leaders.
4. You must value making the connections between the needs of your member congregations and the needs of the denomination you serve.

I want to describe each of these values in detail.

The Value of Indirect Success

First, a regional association leader must value indirect success; that is, success through others. They must find their emotional paycheck through the achievements they help others realize. Someone might argue that this is true in any organization. Success of a leader always depends on others. Successful pastors, for example, are dependent upon church members for success. The difference is that successful pastors experience success *from* others. They participate in the success of the Body made possible through the gracious offerings of members. Successful regional association leaders, on the other hand, are not integrally connected to the churches they have helped flourish. The *only* success they experience is from a distance.

Understanding the difference between success *through* others and success *from* others is critical. A personal example may help illustrate this point. Several days ago I spoke with the retired rector and junior warden of a large church that my business partner Carolyn Weese and I helped guide through a succession planning process. They excitedly shared with me the news: A new rector is now on board who has been enthusiastically embraced. Attendance is up. Giving is up. The church had developed and successfully implemented a succession plan using the (somewhat controversial) principles found in *The Elephant in the Boardroom*. It has experienced a healthy, pastoral transition which we define as one that enables a church to move forward into the next phase of its external and internal development with a new leader appropriate to those developmental tasks with a minimum of spiritual, programmatic, material, and people losses during the transition.

I have a great sense of satisfaction in the success of this church. However, it is an indirect success, a success I experience through others. I am not a leader of that church in any sense of the word, nor am I a member. I have no title. I play no ceremonial or celebratory role. The closest that I will come to any acknowledgement will be the congratulations of a few close friends and the smile on my wife's face as I share my sense of accomplishment over an ahi tuna salad at supper. This success through others is my emotional paycheck.

I contrast this with my work in a parish. When I was a pastor, I oversaw the growth and expansion of a denominational church in an old, landlocked suburb. I experienced the joy of leading a thriving, growing congregation. I was "part of" the success. I participated in and often led the corporate celebration of what we were accomplishing together. This success from others brought me a great amount of joy as well.

The redevelopment of regional associations will require leaders who are able to make this shift from valuing direct success to valuing indirect success. If they do not, they will unconsciously engage themselves in or create activities where they *can* feel directly successful. Let me provide an example from the Presbyterian side of things. Most clergy would consciously allow that a presbytery is something different from a parish church and that the presbytery operates by a different set of rules. The constitution makes that clear; they could not have passed their ordination exams without knowing that difference.

What they may not realize is that they tend to carry the leadership values of the local church into the regional association. In the parish, clergy are accustomed to activities that generate direct success. The primary path to that success is preaching, teaching, celebration, and other forms of public leadership. I hope I do not need to say that this is right and proper at the level of parish leadership.

If they carry that value of direct success into a presbytery meeting, then they will try to create situations in which they can continue to have that same experience of direct success; generally, this means they will try to maximize their immediate impact through their capacity and comfort in speaking before a group. Unrestrained, this tendency spells the demise of the system's capacity to develop flourishing churches as a system.

The fact that it is an eloquent demise is of little comfort. It is the equivalent of that coach who keeps running onto the field and making magnificent tackles. What is needed is the harnessing of the strategic and tactical wisdom in the room for the sake of member congregations. But this is not effectively accomplished through oratory in large meetings. It is practice-based, discovery-driven, and perspirational. Any success is indirect, long-term, and generally unassignable to an individual.

This is why most meetings of regional associations are useless as transformational components in the life of the regional associations. They provide a context that draws out the gifts of those who are most likely to value direct success and the kinds of activities that accrue to that value. They support a leadership culture that runs counter to what is needed at that level. Redeveloping regional associations will require a re-engineering of meetings, their agendas, process, and functions.

For the leader, this requires a high degree of self-knowledge and a significant amount of fluidity in function. There is nothing wrong with feeling a need to lead an organization to success in which you are directly involved.

But if you discover that is the case, and you cannot shift from one leadership value to another, you should not be serving in a leadership role in a regional association either with individual authority, such as a bishop, or with corporate authority, as with a presbytery. Such a misalignment to your gifts will damage both you and the Church.

This is not to say that a regional association leader who is wired only for direct success or success from others will not have some flourishing churches in the association. The fact that they are flourishing cannot be credited to the transformational impact of the system. The source of their vitality will be found in the gifts of a particular leader and the likely capacity of that leader to find resources outside of the regional association of which he or she is formally connected. It is generally the case that vital healthy churches will find the resources they need to support their development. If these are not found within the formal structures of their own association, they will create an informal, de facto association that *will* meet that need.

The Value of Strategic Engagement

Redeveloping regional associations will not only require leaders who value the effectiveness of member churches and the indirect success that accrues to them from flourishing congregations. They must also value strategic engagement. They must be energized by helping their member congregations discern the strategic directions that are most likely to bear fruit for the Kingdom. Again, this represents a significant shift from leadership at the parish level. Successful clergy value the oversight of ministry functions such as worship, music, education, outreach, etc. They find their energy flows from producing and managing a range of high-quality ministries that directly touch the lives of people. If they are effective, it is likely that they are thinking strategically, but day to day they are primarily engaged with ministry functions.

In contrast, if you are going to be an effective and transformational leader you must value strategic engagement; i.e., helping each of your member congregations find the strategic direction that is optimal for them. Regional association leaders who do not make this shift will unconsciously try to turn the regional association they are leading into a quasi-parish with ministry functions they were previously successful in managing. Again, there is nothing wrong with finding your emotional energy though the management of parish-level ministries. However, if you discover that is true for you and you cannot make the shift, you should not be serving in a leadership role in a regional association.

Table 4.2. What Church Leaders Want from Their
Regional Associations: Top Three Priorities

Rank	Goal
First Priority	Equip church leaders with strategies to reach new members.
Second Priority	Equip church leaders to help members become growing, vital disciples.
Third Priority	Cultivate a more consistent hospitality and a higher level of trust between our regional association and local congregations.

Source: *Regional Association Assessment Tool©*

The Value of Recruiting, Developing, and Retaining Leaders

In addition, an effective regional association leader must value the development of leaders, particularly clergy. The research indicates that clergy play a decisive role in the creation of vital congregations. In addition, surveys of church leaders indicate a high priority for both strategic guidance and leadership development, as is indicated in Table 4.2.

Regional association leaders must be persons who find their energy in recruiting, developing, and retaining a first-rate clergy and lay leadership pool within their association. Again, this is a shift from the values of a parish leader where there is a much larger value placed on managing existing leaders rather than developing new ones.

Research indicates that most clergy do not come out of seminary with the skills necessary for effectively leading churches (see Appendix C). As a consequence, the completion of clergy education will need to take place in the field. If we are to develop vital congregations, regional association leaders will need to value the development of clergy and other church leaders. Once again, there is nothing wrong with finding your reward in managing a group of more or less ready-made leaders with whom you enjoy sharing the camaraderie of unchallenging peer relationships. But if you discover this is true for you, you should not be serving in a leadership role in a regional association.

The Value of the Denomination

Finally, effective regional association leaders must value the larger denominational system of which they are a part. As parish leaders, they may have varying degrees of denominational loyalty. But as regional association leaders, they must negotiate between the needs of the local parish and the needs of the larger church. Any ambiguity regarding that commitment can have a devastating effect up and down the line.

As a recap, I would like to suggest four questions to help regional association leaders evaluate whether they have made the transition to the values that are appropriate for a transformational regional association. The first question is:

• *In general, are your efforts ones that lead to your indirect success, or are they focused on activities that offer direct success in roles that are more ceremonial, decisional, functional, or inspirational?*

At the parish level, ceremonial, decisional, functional, and inspirational activities are imperative to vital congregations. The person who can perform these well is likely to be effective and experience a feeling of direct success. At the regional association level these must be restrained in favor of other activities that lead to the well-being of member congregations.

The second question:

• *Are you engaged with the leaders of your member churches in helping them develop effective strategic initiatives, or are you overseeing ministry functions similar to the way you did while serving a parish?*

Again, at the parish level, the effective oversight of various ministry functions is essential to the vital church. Regional association leaders that develop and oversee quasi-parish ministries (e.g., youth ministry, worship ministry, campus ministry, educational ministry, etc.) end up creating programs that compete with the equivalent church program and divert the energy of the regional association leader from an appropriate strategic focus on the vitality of the congregation.

The third question:

• *Are you spending a significant amount of energy recruiting, developing, and retaining a pool of high-quality leaders, or are you spending more of your energy in managing a shrinking body of struggling leaders?*

A focus on managing leaders assumes that the leaders come to you more or less fully assembled. There are appointments, meetings, and patrolled boundaries. Ongoing education is haphazard; the individual is on his or her own. An effective regional association leader sets high standards for leaders but also provides the developmental resources with a "some assembly required" attitude. Effective leaders are not taken for granted; they are "re-recruited" on an annual basis.

Finally:

♦ *Are you working to effectively connect the purposes of the larger church to the needs of member congregations?*

At the parish level, a leader can exhibit indifference, reaction, or unquestioning loyalty to the activities of the larger church. The effective regional association leader must bring a new value to the table: negotiating between the needs of each. The current political focus of that exchange is inevitable but it becomes more strident in the almost total absence of conversation regarding the strategic and tactical issues that could provide some common ground to the dialogue.

The values described in this chapter not only apply to individual leaders but to the collective body of leadership within the regional association. In systems that have more shared leadership at the regional association level, the work of committees, commissions, and plenary bodies should also reflect these values.

In the next chapter we turn our attention to the skills and time management required for effectiveness at the organizational level of regional associations.

Discussion Questions

For church members and leaders

1. Tell about a time you managed something. How did you go about doing it? What made it satisfying for you? Or not?

2. Tell about a time that you helped with a project or program that someone else led that was a good experience for you. What did the leader do that made it a good experience?

3. This chapter talks about a value as something that we do which gives us an "emotional paycheck," or sense of satisfaction. What kinds of things do you do that give you a deep sense of satisfaction?

4. How much help have you had from your regional association in discerning an effective strategy for reaching your community? Would you like to have more or less help?

5. How are leaders in your church identified? Developed? Supported?

6. Do you believe that leadership experience in your church helps people become stronger as persons or actually weakens them? Can you imagine that it might be different?

For regional associations

1. What would it look like if the primary value for your regional association were vital, healthy churches?

2. One desired value for a regional association leader is indirect success; that is, feeling successful through the success of others. List some roles where a person would primarily experience direct success. Now list some roles where a person would primarily experience indirect success.

3. Personally, would you say that you need to be in roles where you experience more direct success or more indirect success?

4. When you think of the way that your regional association functions, how do you think they would answer Question #3?

Chapter Five

ORGANIZATIONAL LEVEL DYNAMICS II
Skill and Time Allocation

Managers are people who do things right. Leaders ✓
are people who do the right thing.[14]
— Warren Bennis

We have been looking at the shift in values that is critical for regional association leaders if they are to develop into a transformational organization. But values are only one component of the shift. The second component has to do with skills. The parish leader who crosses the threshold into the leadership of a regional association (individually, as with a bishop, or corporately, as with a presbytery), must bring to the table a different skill set and a different allocation of time.

Skill #1: Sharpen Strategic Thinking

First, a regional association leader must bring a capability to sharpen the strategic thinking of congregational leaders. This will require a Socratic approach to working with church leaders, posing questions, and identifying issues. It is no longer their responsibility to develop local church strategy, as it was when they were parish leaders. Now they must become experts at helping others develop effective strategies.

Included in this skill is the ability to help internally focused, change-averse congregations become aware of their strategic/tactical dissonance. Every seasoned pastor has experienced this: a congregation indicates a strategic priority of church growth, but is resistant to the changes that are required to produce it. Regional association leaders need high-quality assessment tools to surface this lack of coherence so that they can spend their energy helping leaders respond to this issue, rather than trying to get them to see it.

45

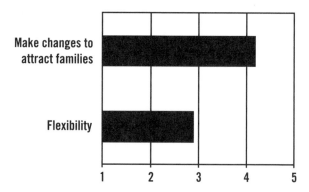

Figure 5.1. Contrasting Desire for Growth and Flexibility Index – Sample Church

Full question text is "Make necessary changes to attract families with children and youth."

Source: *Church Assessment Tool* ©

A good example of strategic/tactical dissonance is found in Figure 5.1. Here we see that making changes to attract families is a very important priority in this church, with a relatively high average score. But the questions measuring the flexibility of the congregation and their capacity to deal with change is relatively low, near the bottom of the database.

While this particular church provides us with an extreme example as a matter of illustration, this problem is chronic across the church. In Figure 5.2 we see the same chart, except that it computes the average scores across the entire *Church Assessment Tool* © database. On average, the indicated priority to "make necessary changes to attract families" is much stronger than the indicated flexibility as it currently exists.

This places local church leaders, particularly clergy, in a double bind. If they make changes, they risk conflict. If the church does not grow, they risk criticism for not leading the church to achieve its goals. It is important for regional association leaders to help local congregations face their dissonance, stand beside their more entrepreneurial leaders, and coach those leaders on change management. Having a survey instrument sophisticated enough to surface this dissonance creates a neutral space for the engagement. The regional association leader is not bringing his or her own evaluation of the congregation but simply mirroring back what the congregation is saying.

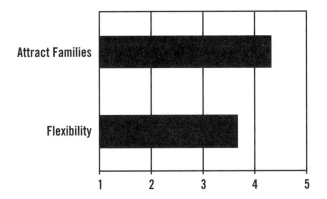

Figure 5.2. Contrasting Desire for Growth and Flexibility – All Data

Full question text is "Make necessary changes to attract families with children and youth."

Source: *Church Assessment Tool* ©

Skill #2: A Portfolio of Strategic Options

Second, a regional association leader must bring a portfolio of strategic options for member churches. In the 1950s, churches could be strategically homogenous: build in a growing location, offer a solid worship experience, provide a graded educational program and a women's association/mission program. 1950s-type mission statements focus on these core functions — and usually all look the same.

It is not enough for regional association leaders to offer a single, one-size-fits-all approach to ministry. Today, churches face a variety of strategic options: community transformation, therapeutic, church growth/personal discipleship, social/global advocacy, and enlarging facilities, etc. Figure 5.3 shows indicators for these different options. In each case, Church One is contrasted with Church Two. For example, Church One shows a clear strategic preference for attracting families. Church Two does not. Given the difference in strategic direction, each of these churches will look very different from the others. Any can flourish depending upon the context. However, all require strategic/tactical coherence, a focus on best practices, leadership development, and moral support. Without the right support, churches end up becoming a hodgepodge of unaligned programs that do not move the church forward in any particular direction.

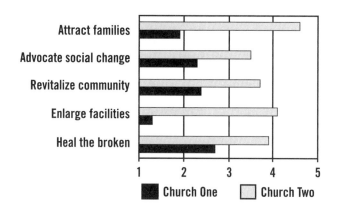

Figure 5.3. Contrasting Local Church Support for Various Goals
Scale: 1=No additional energy; 2=Little additional energy; 3=Moderately additional energy; 4=Substantial additional energy; 5=High additional energy
Source: *Church Assessment Tool* ©

Nor is it enough for regional association leaders to keep offering only what they have directly experienced in their parish ministries. They must be in command of a menu of strategies that can give structure to the discernment process for their member churches. And they must be able to differentiate which strategic options will work best in various contexts. This will require that they invest a significant amount of energy in their own professional development as effective church strategists.

Skill #3: Leadership Development and Training

Third, a regional association leader must possess skills related to leadership development. At the parish level, it is most important that the leader be a good trainer. At the regional level, he or she must be effective at "training the trainer." He or she must have a solid grasp of adult learning principles and be skilled at teaching those principles to others. A regional association leader must not be intimidated by the strong, extroverted personalities that are leading member congregations, nor by the fragile egos that resist mentoring and measurement.

Skill #4: Measurement

Fourth, a regional association leader must establish the criteria for success and a method of measurement. There is a cultural "sound barrier" to break here. Most churches are quick to point out that "success" is not just about numbers — sometimes referred to as "BBs": budgets and butts in pews. They assert this in spite of the fact that 95 percent of mainline churches list church growth as their first and second priorities (reaching new members and reaching families). The conflict around this issue can be partially resolved by broadening the range of quantitative measurements beyond the "BB" categories to include categories like:

- Percentage of first-time visitors in worship (measures marketing and word-of-mouth)

- Percentage of second-time visitors in worship (measures effectiveness of welcome)

- Percentage of second-time visitors who join (measures effectiveness of engagement)

- Percentage of joiners who are retained after one year (measures effectiveness of assimilation)

- Percentage of household income given to the church

In addition, regional association leaders should systematically engage in a *qualitative assessment* of the life of a congregation. This would include measuring qualities such as:

- Flexibility — the capacity of a congregation to adapt.

- Morale — the level of energy and enthusiasm in the body.

- Hospitality — the quality of the relationship that members share with one another and visitors.

- Conflict — the level of unmanaged conflict that is present.

- Spiritual vitality — the degree to which the faith of members is central and consistent.

- Governance — the degree to which members feel appropriately involved in decision-making processes.

- Engagement in education — the level of participation in a life-long learning process that encompasses every age and stage of life.

- ◆ Readiness for ministry — the level of engagement of members in personal and corporate ministry.

- ◆ Worship and music — the quality of the worship experience in bringing people deeper in their life with God and one another.

Regional association leaders must help members break the false dichotomy between quantity and quality in a congregation. It is spiritually irresponsible to increase the *quantity* of members in a church where all the measures of the quality of its shared life are poor. The likely result will be that the quality of the life for those joining will be degraded to the same level of the congregation. Why do we want to invite new members into a church with the likely result that within a short period of time half of them will also feel that they are just going through the motions? Quality and quantity need to be inextricably linked in strategic thinking, and if both are not measured, member churches will not know if they are going forward or backward.

Skill #5: Resource Allocation and Development

Fifth, a regional association leader must make resource allocation decisions that advance the primary mission of the association: increasing the effectiveness of member churches. In some cases, this may mean providing direct financial support for the redevelopment of declining congregations. In other cases, the better choice will be to fund already effective ministries so that they can undertake the redevelopment of declining congregations. Because the research suggests that many churches are declining precisely because they are internally focused and resistant to the tactical changes that renewal requires, a regional association leader must be willing to conduct careful, fact-based assessments that are grounded in a solid theology of stewardship.

In order to make wise decisions regarding resource allocation, a regional association leader must invest in his or her own strategic development and understanding of context. Few issues within a church or a regional association are unique. They are generally shared, not only across the church, but across other organizations as well. Uniqueness is an excuse for refusing to learn. I have found that churches, public libraries, and hospital emergency departments all share similar challenges. There are many opportunities for learning from the successes and failures of others. A regional association leader should model and promote the broad learning that will facilitate resource allocation decisions.

Regional association leaders also must have the skill of visioning and promoting an abundance perspective with regard to resources. Many churches are discovering that revenue is not a fixed pie to be carved up into ever smaller pieces. There are missional resources that go beyond member contributions. I served for several years as the mission specialist for a large suburban church. When I was called, I promised that for every dollar allocated in the mission budget of the church, I would raise an additional dollar from persons and organizations outside the church. And I succeeded. I used the revenue from the church for worthy mission projects to leverage other contributions. Regional association leaders must not only allocate scarce resources, they must find ways to leverage internal dollars to generate external contributions.

Skill #6: Uncover Opportunities

Sixth, a regional association leader must uncover opportunities in the region before they become visible to the larger community. This will require an awareness of regional trends and a spiritual prescience regarding the opportunities that these present. Parish leaders generally do not have time to do the research required to uncover new opportunities. They must focus on the visible, namely, the work that is immediately before them, and trust the regional association leader to focus on emerging possibilities.

Time Management

The final shift that must take place at the regional level is the reallocation of time. Allocations of time at a given level should reflect the values at that level and allow for the application of skills appropriate to that level. Regional associations must conduct a dry-eyed assessment of how well time allocation is aligned to leadership values and skills.

This is not the appropriate place to launch into a major treatise on time management. But I will provide an illustration of the concern. I am working as a consultant with a church developing a strategic plan. The church is located on the campus of one of the largest universities in the United States. When the governing board identified persons to be interviewed for input, the bishop was on the list. The bishop's office was called and an appointment was secured. It took approximately four months to get an appointment with the bishop to talk about the strategic direction of this church. Let me hasten to add, this is not a criticism of an individual who, in this case, is a wonderful theologian and strategic thinker. This is an issue with the system.

The story illustrates that strategic engagement is not a time priority — and likely not a leadership value in most regional associations. The culture in most regional associations has a different set of leadership values, often values that are more in alignment with parishes than regional associations.

Any pastor working to renew a church knows that the issues at his or her door are generally not the ones that are most important. What knocks on your door are specific examples of systematic problems. The more time you spend on specific problems, the less you are able to deal with the system that keeps creating the problems in the first place. You spend all your time and money fixing flat tires when you should be spending your time and money getting your wheels aligned so that your tires don't wear out.

When regional association leaders are not functioning with values and skills appropriate to their level, the result is member churches with in-effective strategies led by a clergy–lay team that is inadequately trained. This systematically and continuously generates a whole host of maddening, time-consuming problems that come knocking on the door. These problems include crisis-level issues around finances, facilities, conflict, and clergy depression and misconduct. If these are not seen as symptoms of a deeper problem, then the regional association leader spends almost all his or her time reacting to crises — and the system keeps generating an endless supply. This makes life extremely difficult for regional association leaders.

Strategic Deferral

Getting beyond this squirrel cage of activity requires the strategic deferral of some problem solving. You intentionally decide that there are some problems you are not going to solve in order to leave time to address the system. You leave your car in the garage with its flat tire unaddressed and take the bus until you can make enough money and get the time to drive your car into the shop (on your spare tire). Or, switching to a medical analogy, you begin to invest more of your resources (money and time) in nutrition and exercise and trust that ailments will decline. Every leader that I know who has shifted a system has had to engage in some degree of problem deferment. Conflict over failed expectations is par for the course.

What is true at the parish level is all the more true for a regional association. The system is larger and more complex. It will take more time to align it to a set of values appropriate to its level of functioning. This means that investment in solving some immediate problems may need to be postponed. Eventually, as the changes to the system begin to take hold, the system begins to solve the problems you had to postpone, and stops creating new ones to take their place.

This makes life easier in the long run, but it requires faith and courage in the face of pressure to solve everything. Leaders always run the risk of postponing the wrong problems or designing systems that don't work fast enough to keep flood waters at bay. But the truth is that in regional associations today, there are too many holes in the levee and not enough sandbags.

Regional association leaders may perceive that member churches want them to function in this crisis, sandbags against the levee mode. After all, these are the persons at the door. However, surveys of church leaders consistently indicate that their highest priority for regional association leaders is equipping pastors and other leaders with strategies that enable them to reach new members and helping them become growing, vital disciples. In one survey, nine out of ten church leaders indicated that their regional association would become more valuable to them if it would help them discover effective strategies for reaching their communities. It is difficult to imagine a clearer mandate for regional association leaders. Regardless of the pressures that accrue to the "tyranny of the urgent," there would appear to be sufficient political support for regional association leaders to reallocate their time in this direction — if they choose to.

Warning Signs

The uncomfortable truth is that regional association leaders may not know how to function at the regional level. A few are quite honest when presented with the challenge of helping churches develop effective leaders with effective strategies for reaching their communities. "I don't know how to do that," one regional association leader shared with me. They are tempted to do what we all do in a new and stressful situation: revert to a previous pattern of behavior that worked. And what has worked for many leaders was discovered when they were pastors at the level of the local parish. Those discoveries provide a useful base from which to grow to the next level, but they can also trap a person in a pattern that will not work in a new context.

There are a number of warning signs that a regional association leader is functioning at the wrong level. These include:

⚠ Engagement in or creation of direct success activities. These would include excessive involvement in ceremonial activity, policy formulation, community boards, mission agencies, and speaking engagements beyond member churches.

⚠ Creation of parish-type ministries at the level of the regional association.

⚠ Excessive travel out of the region.

⚠ Engagement in direct-service ministries.

⚠ Avoidance of leadership development opportunities.

⚠ Avoidance of strategic opportunities.

⚠ Overinvestment in national church issues.

⚠ A large number of member churches with no strategic direction.

⚠ A large number of member churches without effective leadership.

⚠ Regional association members complaining about lack of meaningful activity in their new job.

⚠ Focus on existing issues and too little attention to emerging opportunities.

⚠ Poor meeting management.

⚠ Poor time management.

If a number of these warning signs are present, corrective action is required not only on the part of the regional association leader but also those in the system that are perpetuating a set of values that make change difficult or impossible. Change is possible. But systems will need to become as facile in dealing with organizational level dynamics as they are with size dynamics.

Discussion Questions

For church members and leaders

1. What does your church need help trying to do?

2. Talk about each of these options for your church's future:

   a. A place of healing where members are prepared to welcome and help people dealing with a wide variety of problems to find help and support.

b. A leadership training center that is excellent in developing leaders, not only for the church, but for every endeavor of life.

c. A force for community transformation that works with other community leaders to improve the quality of life in the neighborhood of the church.

d. A rapidly growing faith community which is bringing a large number of people into the faith for the first time and helping them grow as Christians.

If your church could be assured of success in one of these options, and money was no object, which one would you choose? How would you know how to go about doing it?

If your regional association had the expertise to help you succeed with any of these options, would that be of value to you? Why or why not?

3. How would you say your church is doing quantitatively, that is, with the number of persons involved in your church?

4. How would you say your church is doing qualitatively, that is, with the quality of the life in your church?

For regional associations

1. Draw a pie chart that reflects your best estimate of how a regional association leader spends his or her time.

2. If a local church leader — a pastor, for example — were to call a leader in your regional association and ask to schedule a meeting to talk about the future direction of a church, how long do you think it would take to get an appointment? Do you think that is a good response time?

3. Once the person arrived, how skilled would the regional association leader be at helping the local church leader make good decisions?

Chapter Six

STRATEGIC COACHING

*The trouble with the world is that the stupid are
cocksure and the intelligent are full of doubt.*[15]
— Bertrand Russell

The Sovereign LORD *has given me an instructed
tongue, to know the word that sustains the weary.
He wakens me morning by morning, wakens my ear
to listen like one being taught. The Sovereign* LORD
*has opened my ears, and I have not been rebellious;
I have not drawn back.*   — Isaiah 50:4–5

There are many different ways that the role of a regional association leader
can be defined. Is this person to be a pastor? An administrator? A statesman
or stateswoman? The redevelopment of a regional association will require
that a leader play a primary role as strategic coach.

We argued in Chapter Four that regional association leaders should place
a high value on strategic engagement with the leaders of member churches.
This chapter begins by defining that engagement as strategic coach. We look
at the content of the coaching and suggest that it needs to focus on the development of strategic thinking. We identify four elements of strategic thinking
and lay out the basic components of each one. The chapter concludes by
returning to the concept of coaching and what it means in the context of a
regional association.

One of the best ways of conceptualizing the strategic engagement of regional association leaders with member churches is that of a *strategic coach.*
A coach is a person who works with another to optimize their performance
in a specific endeavor through a personalized course of instruction, guidance, and support. "Coach" is an old French word meaning "a vehicle to
transport people from one place to another." As a verb, coaching captures
the sense of movement that growth entails.

The coaching profession is skyrocketing.[16] About 40,000 coaches are practicing today in 70 different countries. The profession is growing at an annual rate of about 20 percent a year, second only to information technology. The reason for this growth rate is simple: people in leadership positions in every profession are looking for those who can help them grow and develop.

When I speak of a strategic coach, I am *not* thinking of

+ a person who writes strategic plans

+ a person who facilitates group process in developing a strategic plan

+ a person who crafts vision or mission statements

+ a person who orders a leader to take a church in a particular direction

+ a person providing pastoral care or personal counseling

A strategic coach is someone who works with church leaders to grow their capacity to think strategically.

Most church leaders have been trained to think functionally. Functional thinking focuses on generating and managing a cycle of activities within the church that are intellectually, emotionally, and spiritually satisfying to members. While strategic thinking includes functions, it has a different frame of reference. A car, for example, has a number of functions that are part of its design: engine, radio, heater, air conditioner, CD player. To think functionally about a car is to focus on how well its different parts are operating. To think strategically about a car is to focus on where the car is going.

Notice that all the listed components of an automobile can be fully operable while sitting in your driveway. However, the opposite is not the case. A car without a functioning engine can't go anywhere. You can have functional thinking without strategic thinking, but strategic thinking always includes thinking about functions. The distinction is not trivial. As a rule, churches excel in the replication and maintenance of functions. Show me another organization in a community that has sustained a cycle of activity for two hundred consecutive years, staffed almost exclusively by volunteers! However, all those wonderful functions can be sustained for years with nary a strategic thought!

What are the elements of strategic thinking which coaching can help develop?

Coaching to a Vision

Strategic coaching can help church leaders with a way of thinking that imagines, formulates, and articulates a vision. A vision is a mental picture of a preferred future toward which the church senses a call. A vision is different from a vision statement. I find that many people have a vision-statement-philia; they are lovers of vision statements. When you ask them to describe a vision for the church, they immediately want to wordsmith a vision statement. But when you ask them to describe a mental picture of the church in the future, they describe the present with a new paint job — and more people.

A vision statement is to a vision what a photograph is to a movie. When you talk with a person who thinks strategically, they have a robust and dynamic description of a future that is more like a story than a sentence. Put another way, a vision is a scene which you can enter, walk around, and describe what you see. Here are the kinds of questions that a strategic thinker can answer about his or her church:

- When you walk into a member's home, what do you observe?
- When you walk into a member's workplace, what do you observe?
- What do you hear members saying about the church?
- What do you sense they are feeling about the church?
- What do you see them doing?
- When you walk about the community, what do you hear people saying about the church? In the neighborhoods? In the businesses? In the shelters? In the art galleries? In the schools?
- What do you hear 30-year-olds say? 60-year-olds?
- When you walk into the church building, what do you see? What do you hear?
- What do you feel?

Once a vision has been articulated in a one- to two-page document, a vision statement that captures the vision and provides direction or "aim" to the people can be developed. It should be:

Aspirational — It should require that the church stretch to be something beyond itself.

Inspirational — It should "sing."

Memorable — It should be easily memorized and communicated.

Coaching an External Focus

Strategic coaching can help church leaders to think in a way that is externally focused. The chapters to come will expand on this topic, but it is difficult to say it too often. The church, like all organizations, has a tendency to project its own needs onto those outside the organization. When it does this, its effectiveness in accomplishing its mission is jeopardized. Strategic thinking seeks to understand the culture in which the church is conducting its mission and how best to connect the offerings of the gospel with the needs of the world. There are several components to this thinking.

First, an external focus stays abreast of global and national trends from the standpoint of their impact on members, potential members, and those we want to serve. Armed conflicts not only create stress and trauma, they also raise spiritual and moral questions. Large-scale religious conflicts often launch people on searches to better understand spirituality, others' as well as their own. Global economic shifts have local consequences in ways that people may not realize. Generational differences are national or even global in their expression and need to be understood if we are to reach a given cohort.

Second, an external focus tracks local trends from the standpoint of their impact on members, potential members, and those we want to serve. Some of this information is simply demographic and can be obtained from census records. Information about the behaviors and preferences of the community population may need to be purchased from companies that do market research. Information about economic, construction, and development plans for the community will need to be obtained from regional planning bodies.

Third, an external focus extends outward to understand other leaders in the community, their needs, and interests. The more externally focused a church becomes, the more critical it will be to form strategic alliances with other like-minded organizations.

Fourth, an external focus is interested in the trends within the Christian church in general.

Finally, an external focus identifies sources of excellence and best practices. Strategic thinking focuses on what ministry approaches are working now. This prevents a pooling of ignorance and reinventing of the wheel. It also keeps churches from the expensive and demoralizing journey down failure paths.

When we say that strategic thinking is externally focused, we do not mean that the church undertakes to fix every problem in the community.

We mean that it shapes all its ministries, from education to evangelism, from worship to stewardship, from outreach to marketing around its own particular community context.

Coaching Strategic Alignment

This leads to the third component: Strategic coaching helps church leaders think in terms of strategic alignment. Just as a magnet obtains its strength from the alignment of the molecules of iron in a common direction, a church finds its capacity to achieve its vision when its functions are aligned. Functional thinking focuses on individual, autonomous ministries that act more or less independently of one another (see Figures 6.1–6.3). Strategic thinking asks:

- Is worship aligned to the vision?
- Is the music ministry aligned to the vision?
- Are we training leaders for the vision?
- Are we educating members for the vision?
- Are we designing fellowship opportunities for the vision?
- Are we shaping outreach around the vision?
- Are we marketing our ministries to accomplish the vision?

Coaching Critical Success Factors

Finally, strategic coaching helps church leaders think in a way that accurately identifies critical success factors. A critical success factor is a function within the church that is essential to fulfilling the vision. For example, if a family sets a vision to provide a safe, nurturing environment, it might decide that it is essential to provide a high quality education for the children. This becomes a critical success factor for their vision.

Different visions have different critical success factors. For example, a church that adopts a vision of community transformation will have different critical success factors from a church that adopts a vision of personal healing. For the first, the ability to form alliances within the community will be a critical success factor. For the second, developing a cadre of skilled and effective support group leaders will be a critical success factor. Different environments also have different critical success factors. For example, a

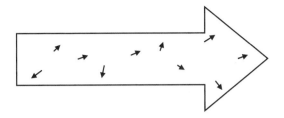

Figure 6.1. An Unaligned Organization

Ministries (small arrows) are contained within the organization but are not aligned to the vision of the church.

Source: Ken Blanchard and Bill Hybels

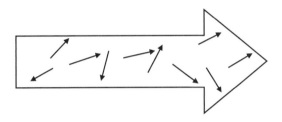

Figure 6.2. An Empowered Unaligned Organization

Ministries (small arrows) are contained within the organization but are not aligned to the vision of the church, yet are empowered.

Source: Ken Blanchard and Bill Hybels

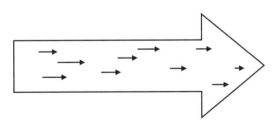

Figure 6.3. An Aligned Organization

Ministries (small arrows) are contained within the organization and are aligned to the vision of the church.

Source: Ken Blanchard and Bill Hybels

multiethnic community will have different critical success factors than a homogeneous one. A community of Nexters will have different critical success factors than a retirement community.

The identification of critical success factors requires knowledge of best practices. For example, many people may assume that the critical success factor for an effective youth ministry is having a young, energetic youth minister. In fact, the more critical factor may be having one committed, trained adult from the congregation for every five youths in the group.

By way of review, strategic coaching helps members think strategically in a way that imagines, formulates and articulates a vision; is externally focused; seeks alignment of ministries and functions to the vision; and accurately identifies critical success factors.

Parameters of Coaching

These four elements form the content of the strategic coaching that should be offered to the leaders of member churches by regional association leaders. Precisely how the coaching relationship is developed would depend upon the local context, but should function within the following parameters:

1. Participation in a coaching relationship is voluntary. It is motivated by the degree to which the local church leader desires to grow and develop, combined with their trust in the competency of the strategic coach.

2. Strategic coaches should provide one-on-one sessions with local church leaders as part of the coaching process. Most of this work can be done on the telephone or using online meetings. Seventy percent of all coaching today is being done on the telephone.[17]

3. Strategic coaches must be clear about their role. They are not offering therapy, pastoral care, or friendship. They are helping the leader think strategically about their leadership in the church. If a local church leader has an issue requiring pastoral care or personal counseling, this should be pursued through other avenues. If strategic coaches become entangled in more therapeutic concerns, this will both swamp their schedule and place them in a conflict situation with regard to other responsibilities that accrue to that office (such as discipline and referral).

4. Strategic coaches must help leaders set goals and challenge them to stretch to higher levels of development.

5. Strategic coaching is not failure-based. It is assumed that everyone needs to grow and that a good coach can help anyone in their processes.

6. Strategic coaches must have the capacity to listen carefully to a leader and understand what is being said. However, they are not simply good listeners.

7. Strategic coaches must have sufficient expertise in strategic thinking for churches that they can critique and offer constructive feedback.

Strategic coaching is hard but potentially rewarding work. Success is long-term and indirect. For this reason, the temptation is strong for regional association leaders to avoid this work by creating opportunities that provide experiences of direct success that are more ceremonial, decisional, functional, and inspirational.

I suspect that some regional association leaders, if liberated from other demands, would not only welcome this shift but would be effective as well. I recently had a meeting with a regional association leader who reviewed the strategic vision of a church within his system. His insights were penetrating and helpful. At the end of our time together, I asked him if he enjoyed this kind of strategic input. He responded that he did. I asked how many other times he had been asked to review and offer input into the strategic direction of a church. *Zero.*

We now turn our attention to the larger context in which regional associations are functioning and the implications of that context for their work.

Discussion Questions

For church members and leaders

1. Tell about a good experience when another person helped you grow by coaching you. (This could be in sports, business, or your personal life.)

2. Tell about a good experience when you helped another person grow by coaching them. (Again, this could be in sports, business, or personal life.)

3. Pick an area in which you would like to grow. Would asking someone to coach you feel like an opportunity or a failure?

4. If money and logistics were no object, and you could be coached by anyone living today, who would it be? How would you begin the conversation?

5. How would you feel knowing your pastor was being strategically coached? Would you encourage that to happen?

6. If your regional association offered high-quality coaching to church leaders that proved effective in growing stronger and more vital churches, would you support that effort? Why or why not?

For regional associations

1. Reflect on the following statement: "It is unrealistic to think that pastors today can be highly effective without the skilled support of others who can help them grow and develop."

2. What are some reasons that pastors would unconsciously welcome, or avoid, asking someone to coach them?

3. What are some reasons that your regional association would welcome, or avoid, coaching the leaders of your regional churches?

Chapter Seven

THE SEA IN WHICH WE SWIM

A two-year-old cannot distinguish "me" from "not me," and, therefore, cannot imagine a world that is not simply a mirror of himself. An organization that cannot discern what others need distinct from itself is developmentally a two-year-old no matter how faded the ink on its founding charter. —Anonymous

The previous chapter argued that one of the critical roles of a regional association is to serve as strategic coach for the leaders of their member churches and that one of the functions of strategic coaching is to help leaders focus on their external environment. In this chapter we explore changes in that external environment and the implications of those changes for churches and the regional associations that serve them. I first want to argue that the church is not alone in dealing with the changes that have been thrust upon us in the last 50 years and that a central theme is the breakdown of single-option systems and the emergence of multiple and competing options. This has resulted in a division between older mono-optional organizational cultures and emerging multi-optional organizational cultures.

The religious expression for this shift is the "death of denominational loyalty." The mournful discussion of this loss is now a well-traveled path. Transformational churches have adjusted to this new reality and accept that they must compete for the hearts and minds of people in a culture that is alien to many of their core values. Most regional associations, on the other hand, are still attempting to function as if churches had no other choices for their affiliation and resources. If they are to re-emerge as a vital force, redeveloped regional associations must shed the appeals to denominational loyalty and make a worthy case for their existence along with every other organization in the world today.

I learn something from every organization I work with. Arboretums, departments of natural resources, libraries, universities, churches, state agencies, and hospitals all have very different missions in the world, but they share two things in common. They are all organizations. And they are all swimming in the same environmental stream. While they are all quick to point out what makes them unique (and what makes their problems unique), they really have much that they can learn from one another if they are open to the conversations.

Mono-Optional Cultures

I try to foster conversations between organizations up front when addressing a group of people for the first time by asking, "What did denominational churches, public libraries, and pediatric emergency departments have in common in 1955?" People are always somewhat surprised by the question because they focus on the differences in these organizations relative to mission.

The answer is that they were all monopolies of a sort. In a day when roughly 80 percent of any denomination had always been members of the denomination, these churches had a corner (often literally) on the market. In 1955, public libraries were the only game in town for information. With no Internet, Barnes & Noble, or Blockbuster, their stiffest competitors were the door-to-door encyclopedia salesmen. Hospitals were heavily regulated by regional bodies called Health Systems Agencies that made decisions controlling everything from how many beds you could have to what kinds of diagnostic services you could offer.

I have used the word "monopoly" in its application to denominational churches rather loosely. More accurately, monopoly refers to a situation in which a single business is the only source for an essential product or service. Clearly the Protestant proliferation of churches has insured against that. No, this is more a matter of perception. In the past, people perceived that they had few options relative to denomination because they assumed a necessary loyalty to the church of their cradle. Like the fleas that stay in a jar even after the lid is removed, they tended to stay home in the church of their parents.

It might be more accurate to say that in the 1950s, we lived in a mono-optional society; that is, a society in which we perceived, accurately or not, that we had only one option on a number of fronts. In reality, we only had one option when it came to library information, electrical and natural gas service, phone service, international airline service (TWA), business machines (IBM), photographic film (KODAK), facial tissue (KLEENEX), and phonographs (RCA).

We *perceived* that we had only one choice regarding another raft of issues: our denominational affiliation, cars (in many parts of the country you could be a Ford or Chevy man, but not both), marriage (divorce not an option), chastity (premarital sex not an option), friends (cross-racial friendships not an option), and occupation (female physicians, ministers, politicians — not an option). In the 1960s and 1970s, people found out that they had many more choices than they realized. They had sex before marriage and lightning didn't strike them from heaven. Women could serve in a variety of occupations — and perform well! Americans could give up brand loyalty on a whole host of issues and discover that the Japanese actually made better cars! And, lo and behold, they discovered they could switch churches. We were moving from a one-option society to one that offered us many options — a multi-optional culture.

Multi-Optional Cultures

The business community was not slow to recognize the commercial opportunity in this shift. With more goods being produced than were being consumed and a loosening of brand loyalty of all types, the sophisticated marketing industry arose that we have all come to love and hate. The focus of marketing shifted from brand loyalty to the needs of the consumer. And the increasing sophistication of marketing led us to greater and greater consumption. We became, in the words of many observers, a consumptive society.

It is important to pause here to reflect on the question, "Is this shift to the needs of the consumer inherently bad?" I believe the clear answer is no. In many cases, the quality of the interaction between organizations and individuals has soared. I regularly reflect on the places where I am treated poorly and note that they are mono-optional services. I have no other choice — and they know it.

In some cases, the focus on the needs of the individual is calling professions back to their core values: people. Competition in the medical field is creating pressure to care for the whole person, not just the medical condition. I heard a medical consultant speak about customer service to a group of emergency department nurses two years ago. She concluded her inspirational speech on caring about people's impressions and feelings in addition to their bodies by saying, "We are being called back to our birthright as nurses."[18]

Many congregations realize that they are also being called back to their birthright as transformational bodies that are as concerned about the souls of their people as they are about their institutional support. This has led churches into a renewed drive to understand people, their brokenness aching to be healed, and their giftedness longing for expression. There is no need to assign pure, altruistic motives to every church making this shift. The apostle Paul didn't reject the benefits that accrue to people doing the right thing for the wrong reasons even to the preaching of the Gospel:

> It is true that some preach Christ out of envy and rivalry, but others out of goodwill. The latter do so in love, knowing that I am put here for the defense of the gospel. The former preach Christ out of selfish ambition, not sincerely, supposing that they can stir up trouble for me while I am in chains. But what does it matter? The important thing is that in every way, whether from false motives or true, Christ is preached. And because of this I rejoice. Yes, and I will continue to rejoice. (Philippians 1:15–18)

For people who do have a heart for serving people, the current culture can affirm and reward that service, again, even if sometimes it is for the wrong reasons.

In contrast, we clearly have organizations that are focusing on the needs of people as a way to gain something from them. I call these transactional organizations. I read an article some months ago about child psychologists who had been hired by toy companies to study which commercials cause children to nag their parents the most to make a purchase. Here the focus on what children "need" is clearly transactional; it is designed to influence parents to pay money in exchange for a toy. The transaction is all there is.

Other organizations, however, are focused on the needs of individuals for the purpose of being transformational organizations. The product or service they offer is intended to transform (in a positive sense) both the provider and the person served. When the pastor of a church uses some marketing tools to reflect carefully on the members of his church and what is important to them in shaping a capital fund drive, his basic value in that process is transformational: his desire is that both the giver and the Body will be enriched in the process.

Jesus teaches that in Kingdom-driven action there are situations where one gives and another benefits from the gift. These are transformational for both. "Even now the reaper draws his wages, even now he harvests the crop for eternal life, so that the sower and the reaper may be glad together" (John 4:36).

There is no question that some churches which focus on the needs of people in a multi-optional culture can be transactionally motivated. But the same can be true of churches that are functioning in the mono-optional mode as well. Systems with adherents who perceive that they have no other options benefit financially from their unwavering loyalty. They can capitalize upon this loyalty to actually prevent transformation, especially of the system itself. Undoubtedly, widely publicized abuse cases come to mind for many readers. But there are many more pedestrian and less visible issues related to simple job- and status-preservation within these systems which are equally troublesome, perhaps more so.

Table 7.1 on the following page lays out the four options for organizational cultures in today's environment. Most organizations are discovering that their future lies in adjusting to a multi-optional reality. This is true for transformational churches. They accept that people have choices and that they will have to be "good-news'd" into the faith. To "good-news" someone into the faith is to assume that the gospel of Jesus is new to them, and that it must be demonstrated to them that it is good. This requires the relinquishment of all claims of privilege and the adoption of a servant attitude reflective of the life and ministry of Jesus.

Many churches have made this discovery and are in different stages of developing a servant approach to the world they are seeking to reach. But as the next chapter will argue, most regional associations have not taken the first step.

Discussion Questions

For church members and leaders

1. In the 1950s you would often hear someone say, "I'm a Ford man," or "I'm a Chevy man." (And indeed, they were males.) Why do you think we do not hear people talk that way today?

2. Think of your earliest experience of walking into a grocery store. Compare it to today. How has it changed? Why do you think that has happened?

Table 7.1. Four Options for Organizational Culture

	Multi-optional Culture	Mono-optional Culture
Transformational values	**Servant Organizational Culture** Accepts that persons have multiple options for their lives. Seeks to understand them in order to bring them to Christ thereby enriching their lives. Makes the case for a Christian commitment that addresses body, mind, and heart.	**Parental Organizational Culture** Asserts that persons can be transformed in an experience of Christ known through engagement in a particular tradition. Assumes that the value of the particular tradition is either self-evident or discoverable through an appropriate level of discipleship.
Transactional values	**Consumer Organizational Culture** Accepts that persons have multiple options for their lives. Seeks to understand them in order to craft a marketing approach that will lead them to spend resources for a product or service offered by the organization.	**Inertial Organizational Culture** Asserts that people need to be loyal to a particular tradition. Draws upon that loyalty to garner support for the continuance of the organization and its particular expression of Christianity.

3. Can you think of a time when you had an experience with a church that felt purely transactional, that you were wanted primarily for your money?

4. Can you think of a time when you had an experience with a church that felt transformational, that both you and the church were enriched by the experience?

5. Reflect on the statement: "People in our church aren't comfortable talking about their faith. We try to live our faith and wait for people to notice."

6. What kinds of needs do people have in their lives today that joining your church will help them address?

7. If you were to list three ways that joining your church would enrich people's lives, what would they be?

8. Do you think that serving others as a way of finding a better life yourself is selfish?

9. Tell about a time you have intentionally served someone as a way of helping them experience the love of Jesus.

For regional associations

1. What steps has your regional association taken to help your member churches adjust to the fact that denominational loyalty has nearly disappeared?

2. How does a church that has adjusted to the decline of denominational loyalty look, compared to one that has not made that adjustment?

3. What is keeping churches from adjusting to this reality?

Chapter Eight

SERVANT LEADERSHIP
IN REGIONAL ASSOCIATIONS

*The potency of love in organizations is largely denied
and repressed. We experience the same fear of it that
we previously did with sex and power. I propose only
that we allow ourselves to become aware of the reality
of love. By refusing to examine love in organizations,
we only prevent ourselves from accessing its healing,
supportive, and creative influences.*[19]

— Roger Harrison

When you have a monopoly, you can afford to focus on the needs of internal clients. What radically different organizations have in common today is that they are struggling to shift from an internal focus to an external one. When an organization is internally focused, the external environment is not even on its chart. As one pastor put it, "The owner of your local McDonald's is more aware of what is happening in the community than most clergy, and he is just selling hamburgers."

The question is not whether these organizations provide a service to those outside themselves. They all do. The question is, "How do we view the person that walks through our door?" If you view the person as the potential resource to help keep your life the same, then you are internally focused, and still functioning as if you were a monopoly. If you view the person as someone to be served and that service may require growth and flexibility on your part, then you are externally focused; the monopolistic thinking has begun to be broken.

Shifting from an Internal to External

Internally focused organizations are concerned that something be done correctly and are of the opinion that the person served should be equally impressed. The reality is that most people do not walk out of a hospital with high praise exclaiming, "They got my blood pressure right!" Nor do they walk out of a library exclaiming, "The book was right where the library computer said it should be!" Nor do most members walk out of a church exclaiming, "The organist did not miss one note!" Internally focused organizations believe that once they have met the high technical requirements of the job (which they set for themselves and others like them), nothing more should be required of them. Externally focused organizations realize that impression is as important as performance.

The shift from an internally focused culture to an externally focused one is painful and even bloody, regardless of the organization. As the T-shirt of one emergency department nurse so indelicately put it, "I am here to save your ass, not kiss it." Mono-optional churches would not fall far from that sentiment, but would substitute the word "soul" as the object of the saving. Of course, the understanding of that saving is to make you like us, which means using our words, ideas, motions, gestures, music, signage, architecture, etc.

Externally focused organizations realize and accept that it is not just an issue of correctness that makes the difference but impression as well. I conduct surveys for a variety of organizations. They are not impressed by having correct numbers on their survey results. They do not walk away saying, "Boy, that Russ Crabtree is one heck of a consultant. He calculated all those averages correctly." They expect them to be correct as a minimum requirement. If I am internally focused, then I believe correct numbers should be enough. It takes a lot of work to make sure those numbers are accurate, with hours and hours of time spent at a computer keyboard. But if I am externally focused, I must realize that correctness does not impress people. What impresses people is how quickly I return phone calls, how patient I am at answering their questions, how deft I was at making the numbers tell their story and help them feel more confident.

Churches are beginning to get this. Leading the effort is the pioneering work of some courageous and brilliant pastors on the more evangelical side of the church. But this is not primarily a theological issue. My research shows that the critical issue for churches is the level of energy they generate among the participants. Churches with high energy tend to be doing better numerically, as well.

Regional Associations and High Energy Churches

People often ask me about various controversial issues that are raging across the church and how differences in theology impact church vitality. From my

Table 8.1. Five Factors That Create High-Energy Churches

	Factors That Create High Energy in Church
Energy Factor #1	The conviction that the church has given new meaning to life.
Energy Factor #2	An inviting, friendly body of people with good relational skills.
Energy Factor #3	An open, responsive decision-making process where the change is not thwarted by the same small group of people.
Energy Factor #4	A high-quality, inspiring, and engaging worship service.
Energy Factor #5	Opportunities for service in the church and world that fit the person's gifts and passions.

Sources: *Church Assessment Tool* ©

research, a particular theological perspective is not a significant factor in the level of vitality found in a church. The more important question is whether the particular theological perspective has been effectively brought to bear to create energy in the church. This energy can be found in churches of every theological stripe and liturgical pattern. The factors that generate that energy can be found in Table 8.1.

Unpacking these five drivers is a book unto itself. The point is simply this: Churches that understand the people they are trying to reach and that create ministries around these five drivers in response are demonstrating the capacity to break out of the mono-optional thinking that is eventually fatal.

The Internal Focus of Regional Associations

Most regional associations, on the other hand, have not made this transition. The same competitive forces that are impacting congregations are impacting regional associations. Being one level removed, the impact has been delayed. There was a time when regional associations were the broker between the local congregation and international "mission field." After all, communication to remote areas was almost non-existent and where landline phone services were available, they were extremely expensive. Cell phones and Internet access have changed all that. Local congregations do not need regional associations to provide that communication link.

I discovered this from my own personal experience with international mission. On October 30, 1998, Hurricane Mitch slammed into Central America, killing 8,000 persons. Within several days, a number of us in Ohio created a nonprofit organization to provide relief. The denominational body of which I was a part declined to participate in the effort, though many of its congregations did. This was discouraging at first. During that time I was receiving daily e-mails from Tegucigalpa (the capital of Honduras) that kept me better informed about what was happening on the ground than I would ever have been through denominational news services.

Regional associations that engage in regional, national, or international mission projects must realize and accept that there are many non-affiliated projects competing for mission dollars. If they are still engaged with internally focused, monopolistic thinking, then they will play the loyalty card: "You should support our mission because it is within our denominational family." The research suggests that this is a decreasing factor in decision-making among congregational leaders. They are asking that regional association leaders make their case for funding by demonstrating that they are the best value for the mission dollar.

Table 8.2 illustrates this trend. While denominational loyalty in this survey does continue to have some effect on the funding of a regional association, the overwhelming impact is coming from other factors. These factors tend to relate to the value of the service provided for the money invested.

Leaders often respond to such statements by asserting that we need a massive re-education of church members to understand what is distinctive about the denomination and why they should not have to make the case for mission dollars. But there is generally little energy for this among local church leaders. In a survey of over 1,000 church leaders, such a re-education effort ranked dead last in a list of twelve options to make the governing body more valuable to them.

Leaders in regional associations sometimes bemoan the loss of denominational loyalty among the members of their churches and long for ways to redevelop it. Even if they could accomplish this, it would not be desirable. The people in a multi-optional society are not moved by appeals to denominational loyalty. If our churches are filled with people who are motivated by that value, they will be totally ineffective in reaching people with the Gospel. In a transformational regional association, leaders will help local churches

Table 8.2. Five Factors That Drive Discretionary Giving
to Regional Associations

	Factors
Driver #1	The accuracy of their knowledge regarding how the regional association is actually funded.
Driver #2	The degree to which they believe that a particular denominational affiliation is unimportant.
Driver #3	The value of the regional association as an option for mission dollars.
Driver #4	The degree to which they believe there are more effective ways to meet mission objectives than those provided by the regional association.
Driver #5	The perception of the percentage of funding that goes into staff salaries.

Source: *Regional Association Assessment Tool* ©

realize that their message must shift to one focused on the persons we are trying to reach and how the Gospel touches their lives.

There is competition in the area of support services provided to congregations as well. Many mega-churches are acting as mini-denominations and are providing curricula, workshops, and leadership training similar in purpose to that provided by regional associations. Church consultants are providing services in the areas of strategic planning, conflict management, and fundraising, all areas in which governing bodies generally offer services. Executive search firms are moving into the church arena and are marketing services that lie at the very heart of governing body function: the calling and placement of clergy.

Even if we lay aside the thorny problem that independent consultant and support services may lead a church away from its ecclesiastical moorings, there is still the funding issue. Churches do not want to pay double for their support services. They do not want to make one payment for regional association services that they are not using and thus receive no benefit from and another for the services they receive from an independent contractor.

Again, if regional associations are in a monopolistic mind-set, they take the position that this is not their problem: churches should be willing to use denominational resources.

This angers local church leaders who argue that they should not have to guarantee a revenue stream for regional associations when there is no guaranteed stream for them. Churches are living in an environment where they have to make their case to their communities every day in a competitive and even hostile context. When church leaders (like board members and clergy) are surveyed, only a third are clearly satisfied with their regional association. Inevitably, one of the factors that is driving satisfaction down is the perception that assessments have reached such a level that it is making it difficult for congregations to raise money for their own ministries.

Redeveloping Regional Associations as Servant Leaders

Regional associations now face a choice: they can continue down the road that argues for support on the basis of denominational loyalty, but they will pay a high price in declining morale and loss of support. Or they enter the world in which their congregations live (along with libraries, hospitals, and mission agencies) and accept the responsibility for making the case that every consultant and every mission must make every day: We are the best option for services that your money can buy.

I will return later to the issue of funding and the impact that a servant orientation has on funding strategies. It is fair to say that this entire book is focused on how to redevelop regional associations that offer the kinds of services that church leaders indicate they would find valuable and could lead to more vital congregations. One of those services is the effective development of leaders, which is the subject of the next chapter.

Discussion Questions

For church members and leaders

1. What services does your regional association provide for your church?

2. What services do you provide to your regional association?

3. Ask your pastor how many requests for funding various mission projects, outside of your regional association, he or she receives a week. Are you surprised?

4. Do you think that these various mission projects would solicit money from your church if the approach were not generally effective?

5. How do you want your church leadership to make decisions about which mission projects they will support?

6. How do you want your church leadership to make decisions about where they turn to procure training and consultant services?

For regional associations

1. What options do the churches within your regional association have for

   a. Consultant services

   b. Mission engagement

   c. Leadership training

2. How well would you say that your regional association is doing as a servant leader to your member churches?

3. What are the obstacles to servant leadership in your regional association?

Chapter Nine

THE PRETTY DOZEN

We rarely see an organization with a disciplined practice of seeking out the ideas of those closest to the customer.[20]
—Sue Annis Hammond and Andrea B. Mayfield

We have argued that the desire to build leaders in member churches must be one of the values wired into a transformational regional association leader and the organizational units at that level. Why is this important and how is it accomplished?

Six Characteristics of Effective Organizations

After 35 years of working in and with organizations, I have observed that effective organizations consistently exhibit six characteristics. These characteristics are the same in all effective organizations, regardless of the particular type or mission. For example, they are found in the most effective churches (of all sizes), the best public libraries, and the top emergency departments in the country:

1. They recruit, develop, and retain effective leaders.
2. They are externally focused.
3. They are tactically nimble.
4. They engage the whole person.
5. They are relentless learners.
6. They utilize best practices.

Leadership is the first characteristic on the list for a reason; it is the most critical. Leadership is in high demand across our society and, additionally, in short supply, regardless of the field of expertise. Why is this? In large part, it is because the environment in which organizations are functioning is in a state of rapid change. Unless the organization has a monopolistic stranglehold on the product or service it provides, it must respond to all the dimensions of that change. Organizations are comprised of human beings and human beings are generally uncomfortable with change; they are unlikely to make substantial changes — and certainly not the right changes — without the kind of strong leadership that effectively manages the processes that change requires.

Too many high-quality resources have been developed on the general topic of leadership to attack the subject here. The concern of this chapter is quite focused: how do regional association leaders carry out one of their most important functions, namely, training leaders in their member churches?

Beyond Management to Leadership

First, we need to be clear about what kind of leaders we are talking about. I define a leader as someone who has the capacity to bring his or her church through the necessary changes that will increase the church's effectiveness in achieving its mission. The mainline church culture has not yet adopted this dynamic understanding of leadership. It is still oriented toward a culture of solidity where stability is the rule and only occasionally punctuated by small, incremental changes. In this culture, those who play important roles in sustaining the order and routine of the Body are considered leaders. Even those who simply play visible roles in patterned congregational behavior receive this moniker. Thus, a person who stands before the congregation and reads a prayer responsively is said to be "leading worship." Leadership as I am defining it includes a ceremonial function and the "face time" that comes with it. But it is more.

In a similar vein, leadership includes management, but it is more than management. Management is primarily a maintenance function. In the church we often talk about board members as "leaders." We refer to committee chairpersons as "leading meetings." In fact, they may simply be managing the various functions of the church in a way that sustains the status quo. Again, this is an important role, but the leadership I am describing is more than this.

We may think of leadership as accruing to a particular office. A person who is the pastor of a congregation or the bishop of a diocese may be referred to as the leader of that particular body. But leadership is a pattern of strategic activity that is detected by observing behavior, not title.

Most of the "leadership development" we provide to folks in the church is actually "management training" or "ceremonial training" or "role training." We train folks on how to run meetings, keep minutes, or submit reports. We prepare people for ceremonial leadership by helping them manage their voice, posture, timing, and text. We bring people onto church boards and give them the constitution, define their scope of authority, and explain to them the appropriate policies, procedures, and protocols. Again, all these are appropriate and important, but they are primarily maintenance functions. Leadership requires more than management. Leadership moves the Body forward; it catalyzes change.

The problem in almost all organizations, including (perhaps especially) churches, is that we have a scarcity of leadership and an excess of management. In surveys of executive leaders, two-thirds indicated that they had too many persons who were strong managers, but weak leaders. Many churches have so perfected the management of scarce resources that even congregations which have declined to a tenth of their previous strength continue to maintain basic functions. This is a remarkable phenomenon. You will find few for-profit enterprises that are able to cope with this reduction in scale — or want to.

But this high value placed on managing the status quo comes with a price. The maintenance culture within many churches is often an arid environment for folks inclined to a more dynamic understanding of leadership; as a result, denominational churches tend to bleed out their catalytic leaders. I would suspect that many of the leaders at the helm of some of the most innovative, inter-denominational churches actually began their lives in more traditional systems that were leadership-resistant.

About 15 years ago, I was working with a church hanging on the edge of survival. I spent some time describing what a leader looked like. After I finished, someone spoke up and said, "Yes, we had someone like that in the church once. He had all these ideas about acquiring property, expanding the facilities, and growing the church." There was a pause. Then a second person added, "He was probably right."

"What happened to him?" I asked.

"Oh, he became frustrated and left about ten years ago."

Over the years, I have repeatedly observed denominational systems bleed out some of their best leaders by either failing to reward or even punishing change agents. They will often insist that they both need and want new leaders. What they mean is that they want managers who will maintain the status quo. True leaders are often threatening to the system. Regional associations must take a hard look in the mirror on this issue. It makes no sense to invest strategically in building leaders only to marginalize those who then exhibit the leadership qualities we say we need.

Once regional associations decide they *want* leaders, they must decide how to build them. I will pass by the argument over whether leaders are born or made. Suffice it to say no one is totally exempt from leadership responsibilities. Whatever their level within an organization or station in life, they can benefit from training. And even born leaders require training to become fully effective. No matter how gifted a person may be, developing him or her into a leader takes time and lots of it. In the minds of military trainers it takes longer to develop a new leader than it does to develop a new weapon system, over 20 years. Building leaders is a long-term, strategic commitment.

The "Pretty Dozen"

What kinds of training do the leaders in today's church need? In a landmark study reported in 1993, Carolyn Weese provided some answers to that question. She had been commissioned by seven seminaries to interview the pastors of nearly 100 vital churches ranging in size from 300 persons in worship to over 10,000. From Weese's painstaking work, we can identify a dozen essential components of a comprehensive leadership development system that regional associations should be offering the leaders of their member 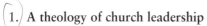 churches. Because there is nothing more beautiful to a regional association leader than healthy, vital churches (indirect success) that are piloted by effective leaders, I call these the "Pretty Dozen":

1. **A theology of church leadership**
    Provide a mental model for thinking about leadership from a spiritual standpoint with a shared vocabulary, clear values, and support elements.

2. **Strategic capability**
    Develop the capacity of leaders to think strategically, articulate a vision for the future, establish goals, align the organization, and put the plan into action.

3. **Church growth**
    Equip leaders with church growth strategies that are externally focused, missional, and transformational.

4. **Change management**
   Equip leaders with the tools required to lead a church through a change process with clarity, sensitivity, and minimal losses.

5. **Marketing and communication**
   Provide the tools for leaders to develop a comprehensive and effective internal and external communication plan.

6. **Multi-level leadership roles**
   Equip leaders in cascading training down through all the levels of the organization including clergy, staff, board members, ministry team chairs, and front-line ministries.

7. **Organizational dynamics**
   Provide leaders with a clear understanding of organizational dynamics including size dynamics, level dynamics, multi-site dynamics, and transitional issues in moving from one organizational type to another.

8. **Stewardship and fund development**
   Equip leaders to assess giving level and potential, to generate multiple revenue streams, and to leverage external revenue through internal giving.

9. **Conflict management**
   Develop leaders who understand the ways people deal with conflict from a psychological, physiological, and spiritual standpoint. Equip leaders with skills to deal with conflict in their congregations and communities. Provide train-the-trainer opportunities to drill training down to the member level.

10. **Volunteer recruitment and development**
    Equip leaders to create a member development system that optimizes the gifts of the people of God for ministry.

11. **Spiritual gifts and ministry**
    Equip leaders with a method for systematically identifying the gifts of members and helping members discern their ministry path based on those gifts.

12. **Staff recruitment and development**
    Equip leaders to effectively recruit and develop an effective staff. Equip staff members to function successfully as a team.

The Pretty Dozen were developed from the data in Appendix C. These are the capabilities that church leaders indicate they need to actually lead the church and not merely manage a stylish decline. If regional association leaders are serious about helping their member churches, these are the capacities they must be ready to develop in the leaders of those churches. With the exception of the last component, the Pretty Dozen apply to leaders in churches of every size.

Weese's research is now about 15 years old. What is striking to me in this list is how little has changed. My experience is that leaders of local congregations continue to be in desperate need of training in the areas identified above. This is not to say that other kinds of programmatic and administrative training are unimportant. But I would argue that church leaders who have mastered the Pretty Dozen will also gain access in the process to the kinds of programmatic and administrative resources that they need to be effective.

I have been careful not to speak of the process of building leaders as a curriculum simply because the word is loaded with formal, academic connotations and the research indicates that such an approach is of dubious value. When effective leaders are asked for the factors that have contributed most to their own development, the three that came to the top of the list were:

1. **Job Assignments** — People learn by doing and they benefit most from training that has immediate application to the work at hand.

2. **Bosses** — People learn by watching others who are more seasoned and benefit from their modeling, their mentoring, and their instruction. People also learn what not to do from bad bosses.

3. **Hardships** — People learn from dealing with difficult situations that become puzzles they must solve and motivate them to learn about relationships, conflict, and about themselves.[21]

It is interesting to note that formal coursework was seldom mentioned by effective leaders as important elements in their own leadership development process.

What Seminaries Do Not Do Well

We see a similar theme in Weese's research. When asked what seminaries were not doing well, pastors responded with the following list:

- Marketing leadership
- Spiritual formation
- Evangelism

- Understanding culture
- Training pastors
- Training leadership
- Teaching management
- Teaching relational skills and interpersonal relationships
- Teaching strategic planning
- Teaching sociological interpretation
- Teaching administration
- Extremely weak on the practical side of ministry in a church

One comment summed up the list:

> Seminaries do not prepare students well to relate with people, understand the implications of contemporary culture as it relates to methodology in ministry, and be a visionary leader. Because of the lack of practical experience on the part of the faculty, the student does not gain a great deal of "street smarts" from their mentors. They don't fail in the academics of their study. They fail in the wisdom of Godly, insightful leadership. The student is able to conjugate nouns and parse verbs, but lacks the skill and finesse to exegete their own culture or be an effective change-agent with people.[22]

Note in this statement and in the list preceding it how many of the issues have to do with leadership, training, and dealing with change. Research from both the secular and religious environments strongly suggests that the academic, classroom model found in seminaries and other academic settings is largely ineffective in developing leaders.[23]

The redeveloped regional association will develop its leaders by systematically and methodically training them in the issues listed above. It will not leave the continuing education process in the hands of clergy alone. It will link the strategic direction of the local church to a leadership development process that aligned with the vision.

In the next chapter we will turn our attention to the issue of adult learning and the broad principles that guide the building of leaders.

Discussion Questions

For church members and leaders

1. What is the difference between a leader and a manager?

2. Do you perceive that there is a shortage of effective leaders today? Why do you think that is?

3. This chapter lists six characteristics of effective organizations today. Using these categories, how effective is your church?

4. Tell about an experience where you learned something valuable about leadership from

    a. A work assignment

    b. A boss

    c. A hardship

For regional associations

1. Look at the "Pretty Dozen," which is a list of the skills that pastors indicate they need help developing in order to be effective pastors today. How is your regional association doing in training leaders in these areas?

2. Do you perceive that there is a shortage of leadership in your regional association? Why do you think that is?

3. This chapter lists six characteristics of effective organizations today. Using these categories, how would you evaluate your regional association?

4. Does your regional association engage in any systematic training of church leaders beyond seminary? Why or why not?

Chapter Ten

FOR ADULTS ONLY

Brothers, stop thinking like children. In regard to
evil be infants, but in your thinking be adults.
— 1 Corinthians 14:20

I would expect that some folks are reacting, at this point, by exclaiming, "But we're doing that! We offer workshops! We do stewardship training! We do officer training!" There is no question that some valuable training is taking place. A redeveloped leadership development ministry for regional associations will have the following characteristics:

- *It will be systematic* — Key training opportunities will be offered on a regular rotating basis that will increase the capacity of the entire body.

- *It will develop core competencies* — The training approach will identify the critical, core competencies that are important to the health and vitality of congregations.

- *It will be reproducible* — It will develop a cadre of trainers through a "train the trainer" process so the leadership development ministry taps the gifts and interests of the body and reduces dependence on one or two persons.

- *It will be "just in time"* — Adults tend to seek training opportunities that have immediate application in their lives. They will throw training brochures away until they have a need.

- *It will be high-quality* — The training process needs to have a good track record with a level of quality that is competitive with other available training programs.

- *It will be strategically aligned* — Training will match the strategic objectives of the churches' leaders who are being trained.

- *It will be on-site when possible* — The workshop model does not work when the culture of an organization needs to shift because one or two participants are then required to return to the church and market a new perspective to those who have not been trained. On-site training can be useful in creating a critical mass of leaders who can effectively lead the church into greater health and vitality.

- *It will utilize adult learning principles* — Adults require a different learning process than children.

Adult Learning Principles

There is now a wealth of research on how adults learn and grow. Unfortunately, a large segment of mainline churches is either unaware of this research or is ignoring it. In my own personal development, I had to go outside the church to be introduced to this literature. The church is not the only institution failing to take advantage of this research. Robert House, a Wharton Business School professor who has studied leadership for more than 25 years, recently noted how rare it is for well-established research findings to make their way into the practitioner's tool kit: "Despite some three thousand empirical studies of leadership conducted by academic researchers, this literature has gone largely unnoticed."[24]

Here are the high points of that research as it relates to leadership development in churches.

1. Adults are motivated to learn when the information matches a need in the learner.

Effective adult training experiences begin with understanding what the learner needs. This is one of the major differences between teaching children and training adults. Because most adults, including clergy, must work a full-time job, they must be highly selective in how they invest their time for learning. Given multiple options for use of their discretionary time and multiple demands on that time as well, adults are going to select training experiences that meet their needs.

This does not simply mean that a training program should be developed by surveying leaders on the kinds of courses they would like to have offered, though that may be an important step in the process. As learners, we often "don't know what we don't know" about a subject and therefore don't know what to ask for. In those cases, it is first necessary to bring the need to consciousness so that the learner "knows what they don't know." At that point, they are better prepared to select training that fits them.

I have found that one of the best ways to effect this change is a simple true/false exercise on the critical issues of a subject. As learners participate in this type of exercise, they often recognize gaps in their own knowledge. Armed with a more accurate understanding of their own capability (or lack of it), they can better discern what training they need and do not need.

Another opportunity for clarifying a learner's needs is to link the strategic objectives of a church with training opportunities. I have observed that the education or training ministry of a church often has little to do with a church's strategic direction. For example, the leaders of a church may choose church growth as a strategic option for the church without providing the continuing education of the pastor, the training of lay leaders, or the education of the congregation at large that will make growth possible. This again is because they don't know what they don't know. They assume that they can be successful by doing the same things better. By coupling the strategic direction of the church with leadership development opportunities, the regional association can first surface the needs of learners and then provide training that matches those needs.

Finally, providing training that meets the needs of the learner requires a communications approach that is learner-centered. For example, I find strategic planning in abstraction to be rather sterile. "Come learn a process for establishing goals and objectives for your church" feels metallic and unappealing. On the other hand, "learning a process that will tap the collective imagination of the people of God, unify the congregation, serve as a catalyst for generating energy and resources, simplify the decision-making processes on how to spend time and money, and serve as a transformative roadmap for community impact..." that gets my attention. This is not simply a different way of saying the same thing; it is to structure the communicative process around a different center so that the experience of the learning is fundamentally and qualitatively altered.

2. Adult learners need clear objectives and specific outcomes.

Adults need to know up front how their investment in training will benefit them. Every training opportunity should begin by stating what the learner will be able to *do* at the end of the session. Examples would be:

> *At the end of this training you will be able to design an international mission program that can spark a broad renewal in the life of your church.*

At the end of this training you will demonstrate more confidence in managing conflict and you will be able to use three different tools for conflict resolution.

At the end of this training you will be able to state the seven steps in a change management process and how to develop a change management plan for a critical issue in your church.

Much of what we offer in the church is theoretical and abstract. Even if we are addressing a contemporary issue, we often do not provide persons with clear steps on how to do something. I learned this about myself when I was applying with an accreditation agency to offer continuing education credits for a training I was providing to nurses on suicide intervention. It was a two-day training and I had to provide a two-hour breakdown of each day with a concrete description of what each person would learn how to *do* in each two-hour block of time. My difficulty in providing these concrete, actionable objectives highlighted for me the ethereal nature of my approach to adult learning.

3. Adults learn by doing and the participation of the learner makes application more likely.

We now know that the best predictor of future behavior is past behavior. When I survey voters in a library district regarding how they will vote on a ballot issue, the best predictor of whether they will vote in the next election is not whether they say they will vote in the next election, but whether they voted in the last election.

(By giving learners opportunities to practice what they are learning, it not only helps them explore their own understanding, it creates a neural pathway that assists with future action) Over the last six years, I have trained thousands of people to deal with the risk of suicide in people that they know. (On average, one out of every 16 persons that you know is thinking about killing themselves today.) The key to this training is giving people opportunities to use the word "suicide" in different kinds of sentences. This makes it much more likely that they will act decisively in a real situation when someone that they know is on the edge of self-destructing.

Churches tend to be teacher/content-focused rather than learner/skill-focused. This is probably related to the importance of our source documents (Scripture, confessions, prayer books, canons, etc.) and the need to sustain the tradition through which this body of content is handed down from one generation to another. However, the Christian theology of incarnation provides a mandate for the flesh and blood enactment of beliefs. Our bias toward the cognitive/reflective gives our educational efforts a rather ghostly quality with learners charged up by great thoughts and no idea how to enact them in the world. But change is possible.

Several years ago, I was asked to design intervention training for churches dealing with the issue of domestic violence. The body that contacted me already had a two-day, eight-hour training that conveyed a large amount of high-quality information on the subject. But when I talked to people at the end of that training and asked them if they now felt prepared to do an actual intervention, not a single person responded positively. When we took the high-quality content that had already been developed and converted it into a scaffolded training with memory aids and opportunities for practice, the confidence level of the learners shifted dramatically.

4. Adult learners have high levels of anxiety about training that require a safe, respectful, reassuring environment.

Adults generally have higher levels of anxiety about their learning experiences than children. Steps must be taken to convey that the trainer is firmly in charge of the group dynamic and will protect the dignity of the learner. This is especially true when skill development is the goal and practice is required. Trainers are required to state and enforce clear ground rules, model respectful behavior, and provide rewards for success for incremental growth.

In some cases it may not be possible to train persons with others that they know or work with. Research indicates that the anxiety level of learners who are in a session with others they know is four times higher than it is with total strangers.[25] Regional associations may need to work at a regional or national level for some types of training or provide that training using modalities allowing for individual instruction.

5. Adult learners desire opportunities for immediate application.

Adults tend to have a "just-in-time" approach to education. They are generally interested in discovering training that has immediate relevance to some aspect of their lives. Once they have received training, they look for points of application that can provide opportunities for expressing or reinforcing their new capacity. If there is a long delay between learning and application, it is likely that the learner will forget the content, lose excitement over its application, or lose confidence in the ability to perform well.

6. Adult learners value opportunities for self-development.

Adult learners desire to kill several birds with one stone. They want to learn skills that help them function better in a specific situation, but they also want to grow as persons in the process. When we teach learners strategic planning skills in the church, we need to emphasize that these same skills can help them in their jobs, with other volunteer organizations they support, and even in planning their own career. When we teach learners how to deal with conflict in the church, we need to point out that these same skills can help them with co-workers, family members, and friends. If we are too parochial in our approach with learners, we decrease the value of the training and render it less attractive and even less effective.

7. Adult learners need to be part of learning organizations with multi-level cascading of training.

In optimal organizations, training cascades down to all levels. This provides a number of advantages for the adult learner, including:

+ A shared vocabulary that improves the speed and quality of communication

+ A positive social/relational experience among learners

+ Support and encouragement for the application of training

+ Promotion of harmony and unity within the organization

+ Reduction in the level of internal marketing required for new ideas generated by the training.

When training is only provided at the level of the clergy and does not cascade down into other levels of the church, it either encourages a dependence on the clergy or sets up a conflict between the clergy and those who are invested in the status quo.

In some cases, only the regional association leader has the credibility to bring a particular kind of training to a group within a church that has high denominational loyalty. In my own experience, I found that there was a group of denominationally loyal folks in the church I was serving that was highly resistant to the changes I was introducing. I remember sitting in a meeting listening to a denominational official listing the characteristics of effective churches in the twenty-first century. At the close of his presentation, the person sitting next to me (who had been quite resistant to the changes I was introducing) leaned over and said with some surprise, "That's exactly what you're doing!" At that moment, a small amount of training cascaded down to another level within the congregation.

It is not enough for a regional association leader to provide a high-quality training experience for church leaders. The regional association leader must also specify the appropriate entry level for the training (clergy, staff, board, team leaders, team members, front-line ministries, congregation) and the levels to which the training should cascade.

8. Adult learning is improved when the training approach matches the learning style of the student.

Adults have different preferences for how they learn. These can basically be categorized into four different styles:

Conceptual awareness	Persons who prefer this approach to learning enjoy mental models, theory and hypothesis, comparison and contrast, reflection and debate.
Feedback	Persons who prefer this approach to learning enjoy the insight gained from others regarding their performance, surveys, "fishbowls," fellow participants, colleagues.
Skill Development	Persons who prefer this approach to learning enjoy presentation modules, opportunities to practice, step-by step processes, modeling by trainers, and case studies.
Personal Growth	Persons who prefer this approach to learning enjoy emotional and physical challenges, team-building experiences, adventure learning, and service learning.[26]

Each style has its own advantages and disadvantages. In larger groups, it is important to vary the approach to meet the different needs of different learners. Since the adult attention span is only about seven minutes, it can be helpful to rotate the training approach among the four styles at roughly ten-minute intervals.

9. Finally, any leadership development approach should make the broadest possible use of resources and methods that are available and that give the learner as many options as possible.

The Internet has opened so many opportunities for inexpensive and convenient distance learning. While this format is not appropriate to many subjects, it works quite well with others. By using formats that are most appropriate to a given subject, resources can be maximized and participation can be broadened.

A list of possible training formats could include:

+ Workshops and seminars
+ Lectures and classes
+ Online training and webinars
+ Videotapes and DVDs
+ Mentoring
+ Print material
+ Videoconferencing
+ Congregation-wide conferences and training
+ Group projects
+ Adventure experiences

Discussion Questions

For church members and leaders

1. Think of the best leadership training you have ever experienced. What made it so positive?

2. What is the difference between preaching, teaching, and training?

3. Look at the list of nine principles related to adult learning. As you think about your church, how well are these being applied?

4. What would you say are the top three goals for your congregation in the next three to five years?

   a. What training does your pastor need to accomplish these goals?

   b. What training do your leaders need to accomplish these goals?

   c. What training do members of the congregation need to accomplish these goals?

   d. What training do you need?

For regional associations

1. Look at the list of nine principles related to adult learning. As you think about your regional association, how well are these being applied?

2. Think about the leadership development ministry of your regional association. How does it do meeting the criteria below?

   + *It will be systematic* — Key training opportunities will be offered on a regular rotating basis that will increase the capacity of the entire body.

   + *It will develop core competencies* — The training approach will identify the critical, core competencies that are important to the health and vitality of congregations.

   + *It will be reproducible* — It will develop a cadre of trainers through a "train the trainer" process so the leadership development ministry taps the gifts and interests of the body and reduces dependence on one or two persons.

   + *It will be "just in time"* — It can be made available as leaders become aware of their need.

   + *It will be high-quality* — The training process has a good track record with a quality that is competitive with other available training programs.

   + *It will be strategically aligned* — Training matches the strategic objectives of the churches' leaders who are being trained.

   + *It will be on-site when possible.*

Chapter Eleven

A WELL-INTENTIONED, FATAL MISTAKE

The quickest way to erode the power of a common vision is for the leader to allow himself to be sidetracked into bargaining over details instead of concentrating all of his attention on identifying, tracking, and talking to the value issue involved.[27]

— David Berlew

We now turn our attention to the question, "Who is a regional association called to serve?"

In a mono-optional environment people have no choice; they must come to you because you are the only game in town that has what they need. You can always tell when you are dealing with a monopoly because they make you do much of the work of getting the service.

I can call my printer (who also does my mailings) and get shipping and mailing information instantly. Or I can call the post office and wade through a phone tree or stand in a long line at the post office window. Why the difference? Because my printer knows I have many options for choosing a printer and he wants to provide me with the best service possible. The post office knows that when it comes to bulk mail, I only have one. It is the difference between a mono-optional and a multi-optional environment.

My friend and business associate Carolyn Weese and her husband, Harvey, tell a similar story about trying to buy a piece of property for their church relocation and redevelopment. In an area where property values were escalating at a rapid pace, delays in decision-making cost thousands of dollars. When I asked Harvey how supportive the presbytery was in the process, he said, "I get the distinct feeling that we are supposed to be here for the presbytery. The presbytery is not here for us." This is what I hear across the country in one form or another. As one rector put it, "I think that most of us have given up on getting any help from the diocese. We're basically on our own."

There is a cluster of behaviors that accrue to organizations that have not yet emerged from a history that shaped them into a monopolistic culture. In some cases, they may actually be monopolies; you have no choice. In other cases, the monopolistic reality is gone and people do have other choices, but the culture in the organization retains its mono-optional values and behaviors. A comparison of behaviors for mono-optional cultures and multi-optional cultures is found in Table 11.1 on the following page.

Now, anyone in a regional association that looks at this list might exclaim, "We can't possibly provide this level of service to everyone that contacts us! We would be totally overwhelmed!" And that is precisely right. It is for this reason that identifying who you are supposed to serve is so important when you are living in a competitive environment.

So let's take a moment and look at a list of possibilities of people who might call a regional association on any given day. This is represented in Figure 11.2. Every one of these categories deserves to be treated with the basic dignity and respect that is core to an organization with Christian values. But how do you prioritize them?

Getting Clear on Who You Are Serving... and Who You Are Helping

When I founded a nonprofit organization in Honduras, I knew nothing about how to run a nonprofit outside of the church. I have long since forgotten the source, but I came across a book that was formative in my development as an executive director. I will try to reproduce its basic thrust from memory.

One of the biggest mistakes that new directors of nonprofit organizations make is that they do not correctly identify their customer. This is because they are usually focused on serving someone they are trying to help: children in need of a latch-key program, persons suffering from addiction, third-world populations in need of clean drinking water, etc. They make the mistake of assuming that these are their customers and that if they serve them well, others will step up and support that work with their resources. As a result of this mistake they pour all the energy into service and then fail because the money runs out.

In fact, the customer is not the person you are trying to help. The customer is the person or group that provides the resources, money, time, influence, skill, etc that sustains the mission. So what do we call the persons in need

**Table 11.1. Comparison of Performance in Mono-Optional
and Multi-Optional Environments**

Performance Area	Mono-Optional Environment	Multi-Optional Environment
Options	You have no other option for getting what you need. When you hang up the phone without getting what you need, there is no one else to call.	*You have several options for getting what you need. When you hang up the phone without getting what you need, you have other places you can call.*
Phone service	Difficult to use/long hold times/ "You'll have to (try later, leave a message, keep trying, wait, try next week)."	*Ease of use/live person/ "How else can I help you … "*
Call backs	Calls are returned after a long period; sometimes the next day, sometimes not at all.	*A return call time is specified; generally within an hour, always within the day.*
Staff accessibility	Staff is often in meetings and unavailable.	*Staff is usually available.*
Capacity to help	Only one person can help you and that person is often not available.	*Staff members are cross-trained so that more than one person can help you.*
Bottlenecks	The inaction of one person or group can block what you need.	*The action of one person or group can get everything you need.*
Attitude	The organization is doing you a favor by talking to you. You find yourself apologizing for taking up their time.	*You are doing the organization a favor by talking to them. You find people thanking you for making the contact.*
Tracking	Members of the organization do not coordinate their work to meet your need. You end up telling your story over and over again to different persons.	*Interactions with you are tracked and communicated to all the persons who are helping you.*
Explanations	When something can't be done, the organization quotes policies.	*When something can't be done, the organization provides reasons.*
Language	The organization has its own internal language that it requires you to learn. You have to be careful how you say things.	*The organization discovers your language and accommodates it.*
Action is prompted by …	Who you know.	*What you need.*
People are kept in the organization because …	They maintain the status quo and don't make waves. Someone in power likes them.	*They are effective and leave a positive impression.*
Justification	You have no other options. We are doing you a favor by treating you as well as we are.	*You have other options. Let me share with you the reasons why we are your best option.*

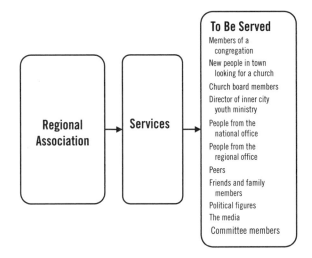

To Be Served

Members of a
  congregation
New people in town
  looking for a church
Church board members
Director of inner city
  youth ministry
People from the
  national office
People from the
  regional office
Peers
Friends and family
  members
Political figures
The media
Committee members

Figure 11.2. Whom Do We Serve?

those

who are served by the nonprofit? They are clients. Customers have different needs that must be identified and addressed, one of which is providing excellent service to the client. You must simultaneously meet the needs of your customer and provide excellent service to your clients. If you fail either, you will soon be out of business.

I know I use the language of customer in this book with some risk. People associate that word with a commercial interest and find its use in the church inappropriate. But the church is not alone; a number of organizations that are emerging from a mono-optional culture find themselves struggling with that word. Librarians have struggled to let go of the word "patron." Physicians recoil from the words "customer service." So do many churches. People object by saying things like, "What are you trying to do, turn us into a greeter at Wal-Mart?" The reality is this: if the church is called to excel in everything (1 Corinthians 2:7), anything done in the for-profit world should be the minimum standard for us. In the depth and authenticity of the love we offer, we should kick their butts.

Part of the problem is a matter of language. We do not have a wide range of words for the person in control of significant financial resources who wants to express a particular set of spiritual values in the world through giving.

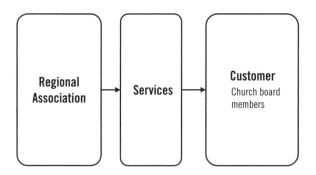

Figure 11.3. Defining Our Customer

Transformational Customers

For a customer in the pure business sense, the process is transactional. However, the spiritual reality of giving is transformational. Both the giver and the receiver are potentially changed. I believe that the concept has value in the church as long as we use it in the same way that other humanitarian organizations of good will use it. In the church, the offering of a resource is never a simple transactional exchange. It is transformational as well; both the giver and the recipient are changed in the process. In addition, there is always a client, always a mission in the world, always someone to be served beyond one's own self.

If you ask most leaders in a local church or regional association to draw a diagram describing their organization, they almost always draw a classic, hierarchical, organizational chart. It begins at the top with a person or council. It then branches down to other functional units. What is almost never on the chart is the group of persons to be reached or served. Potential members are almost never on the chart that a church leader would draw. The primary group of persons to be served — customers — is almost never on the chart of most organizations. The way people draw their organizations is usually indicative of an internal, rather than external focus. An alternative is found in Figure 11.3.

This is my definition of a customer in the context of the church: A customer is a body within the church that financially supports the services you provide to clients in the name of Christ. It may be an individual or it may be a group of persons that has the authority assigned by polity to make that decision. For the sake of simplicity, let's assume that the governing body is funded solely by voluntary contributions from local congregations authorized by the church board. This means that the church board is your only customer. You may have many clients who are important to the board. But you have one customer.

The relationship with a customer is one of freedom. I have the freedom not to carry out the wishes of a customer. My customer has the freedom not to continue supporting my ministry. As director of a Christian nonprofit, I had customers who wanted the project to go in a different direction than what the leadership of the project had decided. I had to allow them the freedom not to contribute. They had to allow us the freedom to go in the direction we discerned as best.

Creating Raving Fans

Now let's get very practical. This means that the priority of the regional association is meeting the appropriate needs of the church boards in its jurisdiction. These are the groups to whom the regional association allocates time, attention, resources, and information. These are the folks that we want to walk away from every interaction with our governing body as *raving fans*. We want to hear conversations at board meetings that go something like this:

You know, I had to go down to the presbytery office the other day to get approval for our bank loan.

Oh, boy. How long did that take you?

Well, that's just the thing. Not too long. Something is happening down there.

Yeah?

I called last Tuesday and a live person actually answered the phone. She asked me my name and then asked me how things were going! I told her what I needed and she said the person that handled that was out of the office for the day, but that there was another person who had been trained to make sure I had everything that I needed. So she walked me through the process and then e-mailed me all the papers I would need. At the end of the call she asked me if she could help with anything else.

Wow!

I said that I was concerned about coming to the trustees meeting yesterday because the meeting would last all morning and I couldn't afford to miss that much work. She asked me where I worked and I told her I worked five minutes from the presbytery office. She said, "I'll tell you what. I will talk to the chair and 15 minutes before they are ready for you, I will send you a text message on your cell phone. That way you won't have to waste time waiting."

Are we still in the same presbytery?

Wait, it doesn't end there. Yesterday I got the text message and drove to the meeting. When I arrived, the receptionist asked if I wanted her to answer my cell phone for me while I was in the meeting so that I wouldn't miss any important calls. She said she realized that I had a life outside of meetings and that the presbytery wanted to do everything it could to support me in that.

So how did the meeting go?

It went great! I had everything I needed and was in and out of there in 45 minutes. And I got a contract with a client who was so impressed by the service she received on my cell phone that she wants to visit our church!

No kidding. Let me check my glass. I want to make sure my water hasn't turned into wine.

Now the reader is probably asking, "What about everyone one else that is on the 'To Be Served' list? Where do they fit into this?"

Clients — The Ones You Are Trying to Help

Some folks on that list are clients. Clients are persons that you serve because they are important to your customer. The regional association does not identify its clients. The customer does. For example, the regional association serves the director of inner city youth ministry only because it is important to the customer. If a nonprofit organization fails to get this right, it is doomed for failure.

Once again I would like to use the example of caring for abandoned children with HIV in Honduras. Most of the energy in that organization was spent taking care of children: clothing, feeding, sheltering, educating, medicating, and loving them. However, the children were not my customer; they were my clients. The customers were the donors with resources who cared about children with HIV. Their requirements were that the children receive the best care possible, that the money was effectively spent with as little going to overhead as possible, and that the communication process kept them well informed about how the children were doing.

On those occasions when donors would go down to visit the project, I had to remind the staff of the importance of the customer verses the client. Sometimes a person would say to me, "I am only about serving the children. They are my only customers. I am not going to bend over backwards to accommodate some spoiled rich guy." In this world there are customers who are spoiled rich guys and there are clients who are demanding children. But these are people with resources seeking an avenue to express their Gospel values and there are clients who are grateful for the opportunity to grow into the fullness of life.

Jesus had those with means who supported his work (and had their own needs):

> [There were] some women who had been cured of evil spirits and diseases: Mary (called Magdalene) from whom seven demons had come out; Joanna the wife of Cuza, the manager of Herod's household; Susanna; and many others. These women were helping to support them out of their own means. (Luke 8:2–3)

But his clients were a different group:

> While a large crowd was gathering and people were coming to Jesus from town after town, he told this parable: "A farmer went out to sow his seed." (Luke 8:4–5)

Customers and clients have different needs. Your client list varies depending upon your mission. But most importantly, a person or a group is a client if your customer says it is.

Bystanders

Finally, there are Bystanders (see Figure 11.4). Bystanders are persons or groups that regional associations engage who are not core to the mission (as defined by the customer). They may be very important to the staff or the leader because they provide fellowship and support. But they are not a priority to the church board.

Mono-optional cultures have lots of bystanders. This is because the customer can always wait; after all, they're lucky we are here for them at all. Bystander issues involve lots of travel, peer meetings, entertaining dignitaries, meals out, and position papers. The reason that the "wake-up calls" from the higher-level governing bodies have no effect is that they are often promoting and protecting the very kinds of bystander activities that make

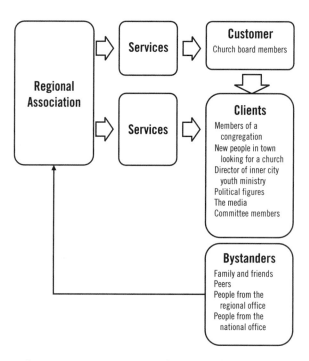

Figure 11.4. Customers, Clients, and Bystanders

it so difficult for first line regional associations to deal with the needs of their primary customer. Bystanders (and their agendas) can and frequently do scuttle the effectiveness of a regional association.

The leader who is able to focus on the needs of the customer, define who the clients are and serve them to the satisfaction of the customer, and keep bystander issues in check can develop an effective regional association. The person who is not comfortable dealing with a customer, in distinction from clients, in distinction from bystanders, is going to have a difficult time leading a nonprofit organization or regional association in today's world.

I want to take a brief excursion here to address possible objections. Someone might say, "Your model is totally focused around money. Does this mean that the mission is defined by the highest bidder?"

Broadly speaking, the mission is defined by the core values of the organization which are grounded in Scripture, history and tradition. In the case of McDonald's, tablecloths and candlelight are encompassed in the core values of the mission. In the case of the church the core of the Gospel is not to ignore the issue of money but to bring it under the Lordship of Christ. Again, the person who is uncomfortable serving customers with money and clients without will likely have a difficult time in today's environment.

So, what do our customers want from us as regional associations? That is the subject of the next chapter.

Discussion Questions

For church members and leaders

1. What is the difference between a transactional relationship and a transformational relationship? Give examples.

2. What's the difference between a customer and a client?

3. Who are the clients that your regional association serves on your behalf?

4. How do church boards communicate their needs to your regional association?

5. What do you think your regional association would have to do to turn you into a raving fan?

For regional associations

1. What is the difference between a transactional relationship and a transformational relationship? Give examples.

2. What's the difference between a customer and a client?

3. What do you think your regional association would have to do to have raving fans among your member churches?

Chapter Twelve

LISTENING!

In spite of the centrality of feedback for system adaptation, most human organizations generally use a very low order of feedback under most conditions — indeed, it is often so poor or misleading as to be worse than no feedback at all.[28] — Donald Michael

...people who are marginal and powerless in organizations may have useful information or opinions they don't express. Even when these people are encouraged to speak, they find it intimidating to contradict a leader's strategy or a group consensus.[29]
— Columbia Accident Investigation Board

To reiterate what's been said earlier in this book, to be vital and effective, a redeveloped regional association must meet the customers' needs, serve the clients, and manage the bystanders. As a first step, it must identify who each of these are. And then it must listen. *Vestry, BP's Corner*

The primary customer is the church board, together with the clergy who moderate, preside over, or attend those meetings.

What do these people want from the regional association? From conversations with hundreds of folks across the nation, over 1,300 surveys focused on regional associations from three different parts of the country, and thousands of surveys from church members regarding their own churches, the answer is clear and unmistakable:

Church boards have three needs they expect their regional associations to meet:

1. Equip clergy and other leaders to reach new persons and incorporate them into the life of the church.

2. Equip clergy and other leaders in congregations to help members become growing, vital disciples.

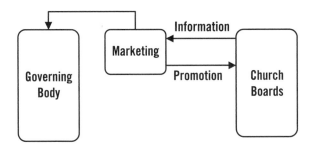

Figure 12.1. Introduction of a Marketing Function

✓ 3. Develop a more consistent hospitality and a higher level of trust between regional associations and local congregations.

If these are the needs of church boards, then there are three obvious clients whom regional associations are called to serve:

✓ 1. Current members of congregations

✓ 2. Potential members in communities

✓ 3. Other clients identified by church boards as critical to their growth and vitality.

All other people and issues are bystanders that need to be managed.

I have cheated a bit here by telling you what church boards say they want. In this book, we will borrow this information as a starting point. But you will need to find this out for yourself in your own regional association by establishing a group that will collect that information. The collection of information about what a group needs is called a marketing function (see Figure 12.1). Most people think of marketing as advertising. In fact, it begins with listening to people and where their pain is. Marketing also involves promotion; that is, it provides the customer with the right information at the right time at the right level.

The information can be gathered in a number of ways. The easiest way is through a survey. Surveys can be done online or in print. An example of a regional association survey can be found in Appendix B. This example can be conducted online with e-mail notification of participants. Other ways of gathering information include interviews, focus groups, and town meetings.

It is important for regional association leaders to become comfortable with the use of technology as a tool for listening to the people they are called to serve. When the printing press was invented in 1440, that technology was rapidly adopted by the church as a means to *disseminate* information. This accelerated the transition from oral to written transmission of information. However, when it comes to *gathering* information, most church leaders are still in the mode of oral transmission; that is, they make decisions based upon the information collected from members during informal conversations. Technology provides the means by which information flow can become two-way and system-wide rather than one-way and anecdotal.

Measuring Quantity and Quality

The top two needs of church boards are reaching new people and growing them into vital disciples. This means that regional associations must assist church leaders in regularly assessing the quality of their shared life as well as the more quantitative measure of people and money. Inevitably, there are debates about the importance of measuring quality verses quantity. People on the quality side of the debate argue that we should not be focusing on numbers, but on the quality of our discipleship. People on the quantity side of the debate argue that we should be measuring our progress by the numeric growth of the congregation. Of course, we need to be measuring both.

Quantity Measures

Most churches generate annual statistical reports around membership, worship attendance, and finances. There are four other statistics that are useful to have if a church is concerned about reaching new people:

1. Percent of first-time visitors from the local community (tells us how well we are promoting the church in the community).

2. Percent of first-time visitors who return (tells us how well are welcoming and engaging first-time visitors).

3. Percent of second-time visitors who join (tells us how well we are doing in bringing folks to commitment).

4. Percent of new members who continue to be active after one year (tells us how we are doing in assimilating new people into the church).

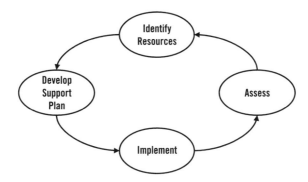

Figure 12.2. A Comprehensive Strategic Resourcing System

Quality Measures

Quality measures on issues such as morale and hospitality provide the equiv-alent of an x-ray of the health of a church. I have conducted this kind of diagnostic read-out on hundreds of churches over the past 20 years. It is clear to me that we now have the capacity to measure both the quanti-ties of persons involved in a church and also the quality of life that they share.

This provides regional associations with an opportunity for developing a systematic approach to their congregations. The assessment provides clarity about where the strength is or, conversely, where the pain is. It makes life easier for regional associations. It enables them to invest their therapeutic energy in congregations most in need of support. Like an x-ray, it helps pinpoint where the problems are so that less time is spent probing the issue in interviews or focus groups. It provides a way to catch problems before they become catastrophic. It also helps identify congregations with particularly high levels of vitality and recruits them as potential mentors and leadership development sites.

However, this systematic approach will also make demands on regional associations that they have not yet been willing to shoulder. It will require that they develop treatment plans and resources for a wide range of issues that they are willing to bring onsite or to clusters of churches.

Figure 12.2 illustrates a system for providing "just in time," customized support for congregations. It requires that regional associations:

- Assess — Discover what a church needs in order to grow.

- Identify resources — Find the resources that will be most helpful for the church, given the outcome of the assessment process.

- Develop support plan — Mutually develop a plan that will apply resources to the church.

- Implement — Carry out the plan

A transformational regional body will develop a comprehensive resourcing plan for each of its member churches and clergy.

What is critically important is not just the information but the willingness to follow through and take action with what is learned. Most folks in churches have had the disheartening experience of filling out a survey, receiving a report on the results, and then hearing...nothing. It is as if the information was sucked into a black hole.

There is a reason for this. Mono-optional cultures are not accustomed to feedback loops and are resistant to taking action in response to them. Action represents change and change is generally penalized in the mono-optional cultures. Change is risky and wastes energy needlessly, especially if you can take steps to insure the continuity of jobs without change.

What steps must a regional association take to insure that plans developed from an assessment are acted upon? Here are eight places to start:

- **Identify a key leader who will take responsibility for the plan.**
  This should be the bishop, executive presbyter, or other comparable position. It should include a plan to meet customer and client needs as well as manage bystanders.

- **Conduct an analysis and restructuring of the "real" work.**
  It is important to catalogue what people are really doing and determine if and how it is contributing to the needs of the customer and clients. This is called *alignment.*

- **Build in accountability for action.**
  People do not do what is expected, they do what is inspected. All tasks related to the customer and client needs should be assigned to a specific person to be accomplished by a specific time.

- **Insure staff alignment of work objectives.**
  Staff work objectives and performance plans should be modified to align with the customer and client needs. 360–degree reviews should be done annually. Staff "fit" may need to be reevaluated.

- **Shift into alignment any cultural rewards and penalties.**
  An analysis of the culture should be conducted to identify points where organizational reflexes might trump meeting customer and client needs.

- **Establish milestones.**
  Break larger tasks into smaller projects to allow for celebration of accomplishment or adjustment to delays. Build milestone checks into meeting agendas.

- **Develop a plan for noise management**
  Identify potential resistance points to change. Develop a strategy for responding, such as Q&A's, scripting, and grief counseling.

- **Define metrics.**
  Decide how you are going to measure and communicate progress. Train people in appropriate measurement approaches and how to avoid reactive responses to anecdotal information.

Discussion Questions

For church members and leaders

1. How well do you feel that your regional association listens to you?

2. How clearly do you let your regional association know what you need?

3. When was the last time you conducted a comprehensive assessment of the health of your church?

4. What would it take for you to develop a plan for strengthening your church in conjunction with your governing body?

For regional associations

1. What process do you use to help church leaders assess the health of their congregation?

2. After you make the assessment, what do you do?

3. What would it take to develop support plans for each willing member church within your regional association?

Chapter Thirteen

SHIFTING CULTURE

Lessons from an Elevator

We stepped into the lift. The two of us, alone.
We looked at each other and that was all.[30]
     — Vladimir Holan
     "Meeting in a Lift"

Numerous examples exist of reward systems that
are fouled up in that behaviors which are rewarded
are those which the rewarder is trying to discourage
while the behavior he desires is not being rewarded
at all.[31]   — Steven Kerr

One of the most important tasks in redeveloping a regional association is shifting its culture to that of servant leadership. This chapter examines what culture is and how to shift it.

Nearly every adult in the United States knows the appropriate behavior for riding in an elevator. The rules are:

Rule #1: Stand facing the door.

Rule #2: Space yourselves evenly in the elevator car.

Rule #3: Stand still.

Rule #4: Don't talk to strangers.

Rule #5: Keep your eyes on the floor indicator lights.

If you were to break one of these rules, you would create a degree of discomfort. Let's say you were waiting for an elevator. It arrives, the door opens, and only one person is standing on the left side. You board and also stand on the left side, not touching the person but standing close to him or her. The elevator is large and the entire right side of the elevator has no one in it. Your have broken the second rule. It is likely that the person will move away from you to create as much space as possible. There will be a high level of discomfort created in response to your action. The tension will not be broken until one of you arrives at your floor and leaves the elevator.

I call this an experience of elevator culture. Notice the following:

Elevator culture has a fairly clear set of rules. Any group of people I work with comes up with roughly the same set.

The rules of elevator culture are caught, not taught. You did not learn the rules of elevator culture in a classroom or read them in an instructional book. You learned them from the experience of riding on an elevator.

The rules of elevator culture are unconscious. People follow the rules of elevator culture even though they may never have listed them. The rules are functioning at an unconscious level.

If you violate the rules of elevator culture, there is a penalty. The penalty is that the other person or persons on the elevator will make some subtle move that creates a level of discomfort.

Every type of organization, including regional associations, has a culture. Nearly all denominational systems exhibit the mono-optional culture described earlier. It is based on the premise that people do not have other options for their spiritual lives; therefore, we can make demands on them that they will have no choice but to meet.

At this point the reader might exclaim, "How can this possibly be? Who in their right mind would survey the religious scene and conclude that people do not have options?" The answer is that everyone in their conscious mind would reach such a conclusion. But our simple analysis of elevator culture illustrates that the function of culture is largely unconscious.

Skeleton, Mind, and Reflexes

It is important to understand how organizational culture works. You can think of an organization anatomically using the human body. Every organization has a structure. This is its *skeleton*. An organizational structure defines what the basic parts are, how they are connected, and their relationship to one another and the external environment.

The strategic plan of an organization is its *mind*. More specifically, a strategic plan is the organization's cerebral cortex, the high-level, rational decision-making portion of the brain. The strategic plan conceives a picture of a desired future and articulates the steps required to move the organization from the current state to the desired state.

The culture of an organization is its *reflexes*. Reflexes are actions of the body that require no conscious thought. Most are not processed in the brain itself and do not require conscious thought. This gives them the advantage of a quick response in situations that require speed. When I am driving down the street and a child runs out in front of the car, I do not have time to go through a full mental analysis: *This is a child. What is the value of a child? A child is valuable because it is a human life. The parked car I may hit if I swerve to miss the child is a material object with value. What is the value of a human life compared to the value of a material object?* Culture has given me the gift of a set of values that enables me to make the almost instant decision to swerve and miss the child.

The downside of reflexes is that they can get in the way of what your mind decides to do. Anyone who has worn contact lenses and can remember the first time she put them in can appreciate this. It doesn't matter how much your mind tells you that it is possible for a lens to reside on the surface of your eye without harm, the eyelid still slams shut. You have to forcibly override that reflex with one hand while your other hand places the lens.

How Culture Trumps Strategy

Whenever an organization seeks to take an action that runs counter to its organizational culture, the reflexes of the organization will react to block the action. Put another way, organizational culture trumps strategic action every time. *Every time!* In 30 years of working with organizations, this is my most important discovery.

The reflexive nature of culture explains why denominations develop and articulate strategic plans that never bear fruit: the unchallenged mono-optional cultures have a whole set of reflexes that override the plan and render it ineffective. This is especially true of regional associations.

Twenty-five years ago I was sitting at the annual General Assembly meeting of the Presbyterian Church. The perennial plea for church growth had just been made and church growth had just been announced as one of the two major strategic goals for the church. Then came the election of the new moderator. The candidates for moderator each made their pitches for why he or she should be the preferred choice of the assembly. What struck me in those speeches was the number of references made to the denominational background of the candidate. *I am a cradle Presbyterian... I am a third-generation Presbyterian... My great-grandfather was a Presbyterian minister...* etc. I was struck by the fact that the cultural value of the system that is rewarded (elected) is pedigree. A candidate who indicated that he had been a Free-Will Baptist until five years ago when he saw the light and became a Presbyterian probably would be unelectable.

Systems that value pedigree generate an exclusive, monopolistic culture that will trump a church growth strategy every time. *Every time!*

Just to drive the point home, I want to shift to another metaphor. The culture of an organization is like a computer's operating system (Windows or Mac). The strategic plan (or vision) is the specific program you are running (a word processing program, for example). You can have an entire shelf of wonderful computer programs but they are useless to you if they will not run on the operating system. In the same way, many strategic visions may not work until you shift the culture.

The easiest change for a regional association to make is to shift its organizational structure. Often, people can keep doing the same things. The only difference is that they are reporting to a different person. It is harder to adopt a real change in strategic direction. (In my experience, most strategic plans for regional associations reaffirm the same basic direction using updated language.) But the toughest challenge of all is changing an organization's culture. That's why you see many changes in organizational structure in regional associations, a few authentic shifts in strategic direction, and almost no plans to change organizational culture. Organizations tend to define a problem based on the least-energy solution. As one author puts it, they attempt to clean up a whorehouse by throwing out the piano player.

If a regional association is going to become vital and effective, it is going to have to do the hard labor of shifting its organizational culture. The remainder of this chapter will be spent trying to get a better handle on culture and how to shift it.

What Is Culture?

An organizational culture basically consists of four elements: a set of key ideas, a language, a set of values or norms, and a system of rewards and penalties.

The key ideas provide the intellectual justification for the organizational culture. A key idea for Presbyterians is "everything decently and in order."

For Episcopalians there is the "Anglican tent." These key ideas are what the culture uses to define "who we are." If you can't make your case relative to the key ideas of a culture, it will be impossible to win.

The language provides a short-hand way of communicating important information. When I worked at Kodak I learned the word "kluge." A "kluge" was a quickly constructed, primitive version of a device that could be used to test the validity of a concept at minimal expense. The culture created the word "kluge" because none existed and people found that saying "Let's build a kluge" was much more compact than saying "Why don't we build a quickly constructed, primitive version of the device so that we can test the validity of the concept at minimal expense?"

The language of a culture can also help a group determine who is in or out. Evangelical cultures listen for language like "personal relationship with God" to help them make a quick decision about whether a person is part of their religious community. Liberal cultures listen for language about inclusion and justice. The language of an organizational culture can also serve as a filter to help the listener know what information to consider and what to exclude. Leaders in large evangelical churches are more likely to accept the language of this book around "customers" and "clients" than many liberal folks who are more suspicious of capitalistic influences upon the Gospel message.

While the language of a culture can be extremely efficient in communicating information quickly, deciding who is in and who is out, and filtering information, it also runs the risk of perpetuating mono-optional cultures by excluding new ideas and sabotaging outreach.

The values or norms of a culture define what are acceptable behaviors and what are not. Again, when I worked at Kodak, developing "action items" was a norm of the organization. To chair a meeting and conclude it without a list of action items was a violation of a cultural norm. One religious culture values testimonies; another religious culture values silence. One governing board values personal interaction and community building; another governing board values time management and efficiency. It all depends on the culture.

Finally, a culture consists of a system of rewards and penalties. These are used to enforce the values of the organization. This includes formal disciplinary procedures but also much more subtle cues of approval or displeasure. I will go into much more detail on this matter shortly.

Bringing a Culture to Light

In order to shift a culture, the culture must be brought to consciousness and identified. This is tricky precisely because it is unconscious. While I have described a culture in the order of key ideas, language, norms, and rewards and penalties, I believe that the best way to identify a culture is to reverse the order, starting with the behaviors which are rewarded and penalized, inferring the values from these, and then identifying the language and ideas which undergird these values.

Organizational cultures develop reward/penalty systems that are both active and passive. The first step is to ask, "What does this organization actively reward?" More specifically, what behaviors does this organization regularly

- Recognize/notice
- Affirm/praise
- Celebrate
- Resource with money, power, prestige
- Promote
- Devote time to
- Routinize/ritualize
- Bestow titles upon
- Photograph/paint
- Publish
- Measure (to catch doing right)

In this culture, what behaviors cause persons to regularly

- Move physically toward the person
- Want to get to know someone
- Disclose information about themselves

When I walk into the headquarters of a regional association and see much of the wall space taken by a large number of oil paintings of all the previous leaders going back 150 years, this suggests that this culture values history, hierarchy, and office. We must not only look at active rewards in a system to discover the organizational culture. We must also examine what is passively rewarded. Specifically, what behaviors does the organization regularly and systematically permit or allow without challenge in a way that can be construed by persons as tacit approval?

For example, I followed an interim pastor who permitted anonymous letters regarding staff members to be read at congregational meetings. The fact that this occurred without being challenged was perceived as tacit approval. This began to establish a cultural norm for publicly expressed, anonymous complaints. Reversing this cultural norm was painful and slow (which is true of any cultural change). I hope by now it is becoming clear why you can't begin identifying a culture by looking at norms. No group would write on a piece of paper that one of our cultural norms is publicly expressed, anonymous complaints. But that was the reality of that culture as it actually existed.

Next, an organization needs to look at what it actively penalizes. Specifically what behaviors does the organization regularly

- Confront
- Criticize
- Stigmatize
- Vote against
- Withhold resources from

What behaviors cause persons in the organization to regularly

- Withdraw
- Avoid
- Engage in sarcasm

For example, most regional associations have penalties that they impose on poorly kept records such as withholding approval or publishing the name of a church on a list of non-compliant churches. This discloses that one of the values of the organization is record keeping.

Finally, an organization needs to look at what it passively penalizes. Specifically, "What behaviors does the organization regularly ignore in a way that can be construed as tacit rejection?" In my experience, regional associations have often passively ignored churches that are growing numerically or are unusually vital. There is a cultural suspicion of "success." This suggests to me that one of the values of regional associations is normal, struggling churches. Again, this is not a value that any group would write on a piece of paper as its cultural norm, but it is what many of us experience as the current culture.

Once a regional association has completed the hard work of identifying its current culture, it needs to ask, what kind of culture must we create in order to realize our vision for the future? This is not merely an exercise of brainstorming lofty ideals. Again, all the wisdom needed may not be in the room. Some research may be required to discover the best practices for a regional association seeking to realize a specific vision.

Once a regional association has identified the cultural values that are required to realize a given vision, it needs to establish the key ideas that will support that vision. It is critical that these ideas link as closely to the core historic values of the regional association as possible. It is helpful if new norms can be seen as fresh expression of historic ideas. The next step is to fashion a system of rewards and penalties that will reinforce the new set of values. The very *last* step is a change of language. Once again, the step that most organizations take *first* is to change language. That is because it is the easiest. The problem is that organizations create new language and become focused on that language when nothing has actually changed. Changes in language without corresponding changes in the organizational behavior make it difficult to motivate people the next time around. After several cycles of this behavior it becomes almost impossible to motivate people to take action. This creates what are called organizational black holes. The cynicism from past disappointments creates an inertia that absorbs the energy of all new attempts and fails to spark renewal.

Mono-optional cultures tend to create cultures that actively or passively discourage risk-taking. I am thinking now about a large church that entered into a yoke with a much smaller inner-city church. The regional association made this process difficult by pointing out all the policies that this would violate. And though the approach was effective in sustaining a vital inner-city ministry, the work was basically ignored (passively penalized). It is not difficult to envision a different cultural norm that would have streamlined administrative procedures, publicized the success, encouraged other large churches to explore that possibility, offered workshops conducted by leaders from the two churches, etc.

Shifting Culture

Once a regional association has identified its current culture and articulated the norms, ideas, rewards/penalties, and language of the desired culture, it will need to begin to make the shift. This will require *practicing* new behaviors. A culture does not shift through the conversation, reflection, debate, or a majority vote. It shifts as people are provided training with opportunities to practice what they are learning. Practice does not make perfect. It makes permanent.

I remember when I was learning to play the guitar. At first, it took all my concentration to learn a basic roll pattern in picking the strings. With time, I became much more adept at the process. Now I can hold a conversation, watch TV, and even sing while playing! Muscle memory is a particular kind of reflex that enables human beings to perform some amazing feats. The development of a desired organizational culture is similar. At first it is awkward. It requires a considerable amount of energy. Over time it becomes more automatic. Finally, it produces a body that is able to accomplish some incredible things for the Kingdom of God.

A cultural shift requires a major commitment of the primary leader of the regional association. It is impossible to make a cultural shift from the middle of an organization. This is a task that cannot be delegated. It requires all the leadership capacity and commitment that a leader can bring to the task.

If you are a member of a regional association in which the leader is trying to make this cultural shift, it is important for you to know how difficult this is. You may hear people complaining. There may be conflict. This is not about the issues in your denomination that you may be reading about in the newspapers. Those will come and go. A cultural shift in denominational regional associations is critical to the survival of those churches. If you perceive that this is what your leader is trying to do, I encourage you to contact him or her and lend your support.

One final note: Whether you are the leader or a supportive member of the regional association, it is important for you to realize that a cultural shift is an all-or-nothing proposition. If you try to go halfway you will merely create a culture war in your organization and your final state will be worst than the first. As someone put it, "You can't cross a chasm in two jumps."

Discussion Questions

For church members and leaders

What is the culture of your church?

- Key ideas —
- Language —
- Norms —
- Rewards —
- Penalties —

For regional associations

What is the culture of your regional association?

- Key ideas —
- Language —
- Norms —
- Rewards —
- Penalties —

Chapter Fourteen

LEADING AND MANAGING CHANGE

*The notion of one certain truth has been shown to
be a political construct, an illusion sustained by an
elite that reflects and maintains its own structures of
control.*[32]   — Melissa Raphael

*Change agents insist that organizational cowlicks
must not spoil the hairdo.*   — anonymous

Redeveloping regional associations will require the careful management of
change in a culture that is change-averse. This chapter presents a general
process for managing change that can be useful both in congregations and
in the regional association itself.

A Great Opportunity

We are living in a time when churches are making increased use of independent consultants to help them with their ministries and are often
participating in non-affiliated mission projects not only in their own communities, but also nationally and internationally. A major international
consulting firm has just established a division to work with churches in
North America. Why? Because congregational leaders are going out into the
marketplace and buying services that arguably should fit within the portfolio of services provided by their own regional associations. And, the dollars
they are spending indicate that their satisfaction level is much higher than
the 30 percent satisfaction level for what their own system is offering up.

A great opportunity now presents itself for regional associations across
the Christian church: providing the kinds of first-rate services that will
be transformative in developing vital, flourishing congregations. Here's the
good news: change is possible. When I talk with persons who are called
to help churches, whether it is with resources, consulting services, strategic

planning, staffing, conflict management, etc., I find that they generally feel that they have been successful in helping churches become more vital and effective. There is no reason that regional associations cannot do the same — if they are willing to make the necessary changes.

Let me say that although in the short run the changes advocated in this book are difficult, they ultimately make your life easier. Why do I say that?

- Life is easier for a leader who has solid information and does not have to guess what is really happening in the churches.

- Life is easier for a leader who has solid information and does not have to debate with others who are making assertions that are incorrect.

- Life is easier for a leader who has a heads-up about developing problems and can intervene before the energy-sapping crisis.

- Life is easier when you have clarity of vision, know what to focus on, and know what to let go.

- Life is easier when you know whom you are serving and what you need to provide.

- Life is easier when you have a publication that supports what you want and need to do.

- Life is easier when more people understand the challenges you face and are more likely to support you even if they don't fully agree.

- Life is easier when you have more clarity about the resources available to you.

- Life is easier when you have a reasonable hope for a better future for the church.

However, there are challenging tasks that only you, as leader, can shoulder. I already indicated at the end of the last chapter that a cultural shift requires the leadership of the "director" of the organization. When it comes to a cultural shift (and the other tasks in this chapter) no one else in your organization can provide the necessary leadership. You can't lead change from the middle.

Change Management

I want to deal now with change management. There are a number of resources on change that are useful, but here is a shorthand version of a

change process that is easy for a preacher to remember. They are the six Ps of change.

Perspectives. For an organization to change, members must be willing to see the same information differently. This requires a loosening of the commitment to a single way of seeing. There are a number of techniques for doing this. One is by placing an image before a group that can be seen in two very different ways. An example is found in the figure above, which can be seen either as a pretty woman or as a man playing a saxophone. Another tool I have found helpful uses the Big Dipper constellation. I place a picture of the stars on a screen and ask people what shape they see. After they indicate that they see a dipper, I show them how it is seen in other countries either as a plow, a wagon, or a bear.

I also use some research on perception which indicates that the brain tends to see what it has always seen. Cats, for example, that are raised in environments where there are only vertical strips develop so that they cannot see horizontal objects. Fleas placed in jars with lids for several days generally do not escape when the lid is removed; they perceive themselves to be trapped even when they are not. There are a number of Biblical stories that illustrate the power of perception. The entire Gospel message could be interpreted as a different way of seeing.

It is important to remember that most people closely connected with a regional association have developed a way of seeing that supports a mono-optional culture. Time will need to be spent helping people look at things from different perspectives in a safe and non-judgmental setting.

Purpose. The members of an organization need to be told the purpose of a proposed change. I have found it useful to produce a one-page case for change. It will fall to you to make that case (see Chapter 15).

In making this case, some leaders have found the concept of a burning platform useful. It refers to an oil rig in the Atlantic that caught on fire. The only persons who survived were the ones who jumped. Leaders must present a burning platform; that is, they must lay out why it is not safe for the organization to stay where it is. This should be factual and clear.

Creating a case for change using the image of a burning platform represents a major change for many leaders. I find that the leaders of regional associations are inclined to try to prop up the morale of an organization by ignoring the hard facts. They keep trying to look on the bright side, give positive anecdotal accounts, and look at the half-full glass. This merely postpones the facing of painful realities. It fosters an environment where persons are individually anxious but pretend to be positive as a group.

The presentation of the purpose for a change does not have to be negative as long as there is also a . . .

Picture. That is, a picture of a preferred future. You are not asking people to jump into a nameless abyss. You are painting for them a vision of what the future will look like. This not only includes a description of what will change; it also includes as clear a description of what will not change. Wherever possible, try to tie into the history of the body to show how what you are asking of them is consistent with past values and behavior.

Once people have in mind a clear picture of a preferred future, then you can work with them to develop the . . .

Plan. If the Purpose describes where the organization is (on the burning platform) and the Picture describes the future, the Plan describes the step-by-step process by which the organization is going to move into the future. This needs to include all the critical elements of the organization's life, including staff, program, finances, property, and culture. While you as leader will need to play the leading role in developing the Picture, other members can be brought in to generate the elements of the plan.

By doing so you begin to build . . .

Participation. Participation breeds commitment. It is important to let people know the variety of ways they can participate in the change process. This is a great opportunity to bring members of the congregation on board. Since you are shifting the focus of your regional association's work to better serve them, ask for their prayers and engagement. Form focus groups, conduct interviews, encourage book studies (including the study of this book), solicit prayers, or commission art, music, and drama.

And of course, we have to remember that people are going to react emotionally to change, so we have to deal with...

Psychology. Try to anticipate where people are going to lose the most in the change process. Articulate those losses. You are going to experience loss in the process, too. Be sure to articulate your losses as well. Recruit persons with pastoral skills to listen to people in some structured meetings.

Diffusion of Innovation

One of the most helpful concepts I have found in thinking about change management (and fundraising, as well) is a concept called the diffusion of innovation (see Figure 14.1).[33] The basic idea is that people get on board with new ideas at different points in the process and that they have different requirements for getting on board. "Pioneers" (people like you!) need only a compelling vision to get on board. They represent a relatively small percentage of your regional association. You need to find them and solicit their support first.

The next group to get on board is called "early adopters." There are more persons in this group and they should be easier to find. In order for them to get on board they need to have a compelling vision, but they also need to see that the pioneers are on board, too. If you were to go straight to the early adopters and skip bringing the pioneers on board, you are going to lose some support.

The next group to get on board is called the "early majority." This is a fairly large group; about a third of an organization falls in this category. They need to see the compelling vision and the pioneers and early adopters on board. But they also need to see some early success of the idea.

The "late majority" is about the same size as the early majority. They need to see everything the early majority sees, accompanied by some multiple successes. The "skittish supporters" will never be fully on board.

This chart is not simply interesting information about how people deal with change. It suggests a strategy for bringing about change and demonstrates why the same innovation presented in different ways can either succeed or fail. For example, if you include the skittish supporters and the later majority too soon, they can introduce enough anxiety to scuttle the process. However, if you are careful to cultivate the pioneers, early adopters,

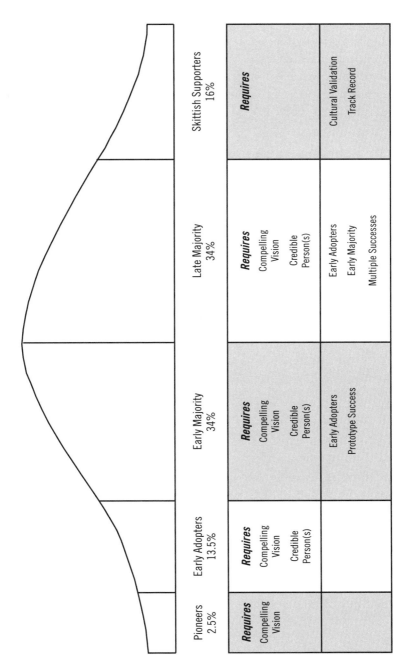

Figure 14.1. Diffusion of Innovation: How People Get on Board with New Ideas

and early majority first, the other groups are much more likely to come along.

It is helpful to identify the pioneers in your organization and get them on board. You can then brainstorm with them regarding the early adopters that they know and charge them with the responsibility of helping you win their support. With those folks behind you, you can then brainstorm with them about the next group, and so on.

Managing A-Team and B-Team Behavior

One of your tasks as a leader is working to insure that negative, dysfunctional behaviors do not sabotage the work of your regional association. While you can train other persons to do this, you have to take the initiative. It is risky enough that your followers need to know that you are with them.

One of the most powerful tools I have found in dealing with problematic behaviors is that of A-Teams and B-Teams.[34] It is especially helpful when folks are exhibiting dysfunctional behaviors. It works every time I use it. Here's how the exercise goes:

"Say, do you ever find yourself wanting to go to some meetings more than others? What do you think makes the difference?

"I think I know one important answer to that question. Have you ever gone to a committee meeting for the first time and when you see who is there, you say to yourself, 'Bring it on. With this group of people we can do anything.' "

People will generally nod in agreement.

How would you describe that group of people? Well, I have asked that question all over the country and the answer is the same. They are

- Positive

- Communicative

- Initiators

- Good sense of humor

- Flexible

- Can-do attitude

We call these folks "the A-Team."

"Next question. Have you ever gone to a meeting for the first time, seen who was there and said to yourself, *'Shoot me now.'* Of course you have."

How would you describe that group of people? Well, again, I have asked that question all over the country and the answer is the same. They are

+ Negative

+ Out of the loop

+ Don't laugh

+ Anxious about doing anything

+ Rigid

+ Don't understand

We call these folks "the B-Team."

"OK. Everyone with me? Now, here is the final question: How many B-Team people does it take to sink the morale of an entire A-Team?

"Right! *One!* So one of the most important things we need to be able to do to keep the morale of our regional association up is to learn how to deal with B-Team behavior. Sometimes that will mean talking into the mirror. And sometimes it will mean talking to other people. But that's what I am going to train you all to do."

Training people to deal with A- and B-Team behavior is an important task. When people are equipped to do that, the system becomes self-regulating and less dependent upon the leader to keep the organization healthy and vital.

Discussion Questions

For church members and leaders

1. Think about a major change that your church went through in the last five years. How did your congregation deal with that change?

2. Think of a scenario in which your church might take a positive step that would involve a major amount of change.

    a. How would you help people to look at it differently (shift perception)?

    b. How would you explain to people why it is important not to stay where you are; that is, not make the change (state purpose)?

c. How would you describe the future after the change was made (paint picture)?

d. How would you go about forming a step-by-step process to effect the change (develop plan)?

e. How might you get as many people as possible involved (build participation)?

f. How would you help people deal with their emotions about the change (psychology)?

For regional associations

Use questions #1 and #2 above, but apply them to your regional association.

Chapter Fifteen

STRAIGHT TALK

You will know the truth and the truth shall set you free. But first it will make you miserable.
— Refrigerator poster

As stated in Chapter One, denominational leaders often send a mixed message regarding the state of the church. On the one hand, they issue wake-up calls about the need for church, potentially creating impetus for change. This impetus is then blunted by an "on the other hand" message explaining why things are not as bad as they appear. The more we are asking of people, the clearer we must be about the imperative for action. It is an abuse of leadership to ask people to walk through the discomfort of change on one day and imply that it is unnecessary on the next.

The redevelopment of a regional association requires that leaders exhibit a clear, consistent pattern of communication skills. In situations that call for significant change, clear communication makes or breaks the process. In this chapter I submit that our reasons for change must be considered from an external standpoint. Then I look at the need to create a case for change. I suggest that leaders avoid the "on the one hand/on the other hand" communication approach. I then look at the need to communicate best practices. I close with a few comments on what makes for high morale within an organization.

An External Focus to the Message

In mono-optional church cultures, the need for change is often communicated from an internal perspective: we are losing members, we need more money, there is too much work for a few of us to do, etc. If the culture is to be shifted, it is important to communicate the need for change from an external, missional perspective. That message is simply this: We are failing to offer the world the message of a Gospel that is lifesaving and a Gospel community that is soul-safe. Our message to the world tends to be more focused on the noble qualities of our church tradition, not on the power of the Gospel to transform lives. The quality of community that we offer to the world is often spiritually and emotionally unsafe. Nearly one in three staff members in regional associations agree or tend to agree that their work is making it harder for them to have a vital spiritual life. As stated earlier, inviting people into a church community where the research indicates it likely that they will end up feeling that they are just going through the motions is spiritually reprehensible.

The deeper message is not that we must change or our churches will close; it is that we are failing one another, failing the world, failing our God, and betraying the beauty and wonder of the Gospel by the way we are living. This is a call to repentance in both the Hebrew perspective (change your behavior) and the Greek perspective (change your mind). The redevelopment of a regional association into a transformational organization is a corporate and individual act of repentance.

What steps must a regional association leader take to insure clear communication around critical issues? What follows falls far short of a comprehensive communication strategy. Instead, I want to focus on specific issues where I have seen a chronic confusion make it nearly impossible for people to know how to follow.

1. Create a concise, compelling, evidence-based, and consistently communicated case for change that articulates why your regional association cannot stay where it is.

By concise, I mean one or two pages.

By compelling, I mean that it addresses the motivational factors within the listener, namely

- It is consistent with their core values.
- It builds on their previous and therefore most predictable behaviors.
- It provides a benefit that has worth to them.
- It connects them to others they respect and tend to follow.
- It demonstrates uniqueness and urgency in its approach.

By evidence-based, I mean that it builds on commonly accessible facts that are beyond reasonable dispute, rather than guesses, opinions, or concepts.

By consistently communicated, I mean that it is offered in a variety of formats — electronic, print, DVD, and CD. But more importantly, it is memorized by every leader within the regional association and can be delivered as a five-minute stump speech on demand. *Consistently* means that the leader does not present the imperative for change in one context and then try to prop up morale with a "look at the bright side" speech in another.

2. Avoid the use of on-the-one-hand, on-the-other-hand reports on how your regional association is doing.

This problematic type of reporting takes many forms.

- This has been a year of highs and lows...

- My report will focus on some of the joys but also some of the sorrows...

- This year has seen some gains and some losses...

- One could look at our situation as either the cup is half-empty or half-full...

- In my report I am going to highlight some positives and some negatives...

Whatever form it takes, this approach to communicating the status of an organization tends to produce pluses and minuses that null one another out, create emotional flat spots, and arrest movement. People often say they are seeking to be balanced. While striving for balance feels admirable, you don't want balance. You want change.

These on-the-one-hand, on-the-other-hand assessments encourage the fallacy of the average experience. It is this fallacy that enables people to list three positives in the statistics of the church, then list three negatives, and conclude that, on the whole, things are OK; we simply need to continue doing what we have always done. In over 30 years of working in denominational systems, I have seen this approach used repeatedly to reinforce the status quo. It has the exact opposite effect of making a case for change; if a case for change exists, it guts it of real impact.

On-the-one-hand, on-the-other-hand assessments also encourage the fallacy of equal factors. It is this fallacy that makes good-news/bad-news jokes so funny because they assume that a really trivial piece of "good news" (your husband's surgery went faster than we expected) can compensate for a really major piece of "bad news" (his heart stopped in the first five minutes of the operation). This actually dumbs down the problem-solving capacity of the body by encouraging members to focus on issues that are of little strategic consequence ("majoring in minors") and ignoring issues that are pivotal (the "big rocks in the jar").

Looking for good news to balance bad news in reports undermines the entire case for change. Instead of focusing on balance, reports should focus on progress, or lack of it, in moving toward desired change. A report using this approach might begin:

> I would like to share with you the progress we have made this year in implementing the changes that we agreed are essential to our future vitality and effectiveness. We have ten critical changes that we indicated we wanted to make in the last year. We have succeeded in seven of those areas. I want to share those successes with you and the plans we have to build on and expand those successes. We have fallen short in three of those areas. These remain critical to our vision and I want to share with you the steps that we are taking to address them.

Where progress is present, it should be celebrated and advanced; where progress is absent remedial action should be planned and implemented. But this will require that you . . .

3. Utilize best practices to identify and then communicate the factors most critical to realizing your vision.

Not every action is of equal value in realizing a vision and the actual importance of an action may not be intuitively obvious. There is a substantial amount of research demonstrating that the general public misjudges the magnitude of a number of issues in trying to solve a problem. For example, when it comes to balancing the federal budget most people markedly overestimate the amount of money in the budget that goes to welfare and foreign aid while underestimating the amount of the budget spent on social security (see Table 15.1).[35]

In fact, the public has it precisely upside down: the item that is considered to be the largest (foreign aid) is actually the smallest and the item that is considered to the smallest (Social Security) is actually the largest. This factual example illustrates that without proper training, people will often *overestimate* how critical one factor is in solving a problem and *underestimate* how critical another factor is in solving the same problem. If the public is so misinformed about matters so general and information so readily available, there is no reason to be confident that church folks will be better informed regarding the practices of effective ministry unless there is an intentional, sustained effort to train them.

Accurately discerning the critical success factors for realizing a vision and effectively communicating them are two of the most important tasks of a regional association leader.

Table 15.1. Americans' Views of the Two Largest Areas
of Federal Government Spending

Item	Percentage Selecting Area as *One of the Two Largest Areas of Federal Spending*	Actual Federal Budget Share
Foreign Aid	41%	1.2%
Welfare	40%	10.2%
Defense	37%	20.7%
Social Security	14%	21.6%

In my experience, I find that most regional association leaders over-estimate

- their ability to brainstorm their way to effective strategies without training (the wisdom is in the room);
- the value of their particular denominational tradition to people in the community ("If we can get people to see what makes our tradition special, they will see why they should be involved with us");
- the power of cognitive changes to effect behavioral changes ("We can think ourselves into a new way of acting");
- the power of hospitality to generate high morale in their regional association.

Conversely, I find that most regional association leaders underestimate

- the need for a significant marketing effort aimed at local church leaders;
- the hunger of local church leaders for high quality, proven resources;
- their potential strategic impact on churches searching for direction.

Regional association leaders cannot assume that they or the well-intentioned people they lead have the necessary training to realize a vision. They need to procure the expertise required to skillfully identify the critical success factors in their particular context, train their people on how to address them, and stay focused on them through a clear, consistent communication process.

Churches often set strategic goals ("We will increase our membership by 200 members over the next five years."). Strategic goals (people, budgets, buildings) are useless if you are not identifying and addressing the factors required in getting there. Regional association leaders must help identify and communicate these factors.

As incredible as it may seem, one overlooked source of best practices within regional associations are those who have developed healthy, vital churches. In the assessment process I will occasionally turn up transformational churches that have developed a markedly different quality of congregational life. When I ask the pastor how many times they have been asked by their regional association to share what they have learned, the answer is always, without exception, the same: *zero*! As much as we may talk about being connectional, regional associations have cultures that passively reward self-containment and passively punish effectiveness. Shifting this culture to one that rewards teachability, trust, and best practices is one of the most important tasks of the leadership in a transformational regional association.

4. Finally, understand and put into practice the mechanisms that make for high morale.

This may not appear to fit in a chapter dealing with communication. I place it at this point because leaders often overestimate the impact of "positive spin" on generating high morale. This places them in a bind: they realize the need for change and want to communicate that need, but they are afraid to tell the truth for fear that it will damage morale and make life even harder. So they fall into the trap of "looking at the bright side" which, as I have said, undermines the case for change. Or they try to improve morale by creating more "Kum Ba Yah" experiences that may only marginally impact morale.

Regional association leaders have the complex task of maintaining the morale of the organization as well as that of staff members who serve the association. Staff survey results found in Table 15.2 show a high percentage of respondents on the fence on issues such as teamwork, effective use of meetings, and the impact of their work on their spiritual lives. When asked what would most likely improve their work effectiveness and job satisfaction, their top three priorities focused on communication, personal development, and technology (Table 15.3).

The factors in generating high morale in an organization are well known and understood. These factors are divided into two categories: baseline and premium.

Baseline morale factors are those that must be effectively addressed to bring morale to a basic, minimal level. Baseline morale factors can never

Table 15.2. Survey Results for Regional Association Staff Members

Survey Item	Clearly Not	On the Fence	Clearly Yes
Trained to work as team	17%	53%	30%
Meetings used effectively	8%	51%	41%
Disturbed by conflict	52%	37%	11%
Work fair and balanced	6%	48%	46%
Someone has talked to me about progress	35%	35%	31%
Work makes spiritual life hard	41%	49%	10%

Sources: *Regional Association Staff Assessment Tool* ©

Table 15.3. What Is Most Likely to Improve Work Effectiveness

Priority Type	Unlikely/ Very Unlikely	Likely	Very Likely
Improve communication	4%	52%	44%
More opportunities for professional development	4%	52%	44%
Equip staff with technology	8%	52%	40%

Sources: *Regional Association Staff Assessment Tool* ©

generate high morale; they simply keep you from having low morale. An analogy would be changing the oil in your car. Changing the oil in your car will never give you a great vacation. But if the engine blows up because the oil has not been changed, it can virtually guarantee a bad vacation.

Baseline morale factors include the following:

1. Church policy and administration is fair and reasonable.

2. Leadership is competent and appropriate to the position.

3. There is a positive relationship between leaders and followers.

4. Physical conditions are conducive to productivity.

5. Relationship with peers is positive and constructive.

6. Concern is expressed for the member's personal life.

7. Leaders have a good relationship with those they lead.

8. Compensation is fair and competitive.

Once again, these are minimal requirements. If baseline morale factors are not effectively addressed they can lead to low morale. Once they are in place, doing more with them will not provide for high morale. Higher salaries do not make for the highest morale. They merely lead to people saying, "I hate this job, but I can't afford to quit it." Improving relationships does not make for the highest morale. It merely leads to "the people are nice but I don't feel like we are accomplishing anything."

So, what is the source of high morale in an organization? Premium morale factors generate high morale; the more the better. These include the following:

1. Members are engaged in ministry that matches their talent, skill, knowledge, and interests.

2. Members have opportunities to make significant achievements.

3. Members are recognized for work well done.

4. Members are provided with opportunities for personal and professional growth.

If these twelve factors are effectively addressed, organizational morale will tend to be high, even when a difficult truth must be faced. If these twelve factors are neglected, low morale is inevitable and no amount of lipstick on the pig will win the heart of the suitor.

Discussion Questions

For church members and leaders

1. State why people should join your church

   a. From an internal perspective

   b. From an external perspective

2. Look at the overall quality of the community experience of people in your church. If new members came to reflect that experience, would the quality of their lives improve or decline?

3. Is the need for change being communicated in your church? How is it being done?

For regional associations

1. What case for change would you make for redeveloping your regional association?

2. Look at the overall quality of the leadership experience in your regional association. If new leaders came to reflect that experience, would the quality of their lives improve or decline?

3. About a third of regional association staff members indicate that their work tends to make it difficult for them to have a vital spiritual life. Do you think that is the case for your staff members? What do you think can be done about that?

Chapter Sixteen

IN THE SCHOOL OF THE INVOICE

Anecdotal stories become operating facts when told
often enough and when an organization does not
take the time to question underlying assumptions.[36]
— Sue Annis Hammond and Andrea B. Mayfield

A number of years ago, when I was still a pastor, I learned something while I was paying my obligatory visit to the finance committee. The group was wrestling with the issue of another committee chairperson who would not submit her bills for payment on time. As a result, the church was incurring late fees, not to mention the negative impression regarding the Christian community left with the vendor. A number of potential solutions was proposed, all of which had been tried. Finally, one of the members said, "I think we should send her a bill for the late fee. Nothing educates like an invoice."

The mono-optional culture is slow to respond to indicators that it is losing ground. When nothing else seems instructive, money begins to teach. I call it the school of the invoice. Unfortunately, we have not exactly been honor students.

As it became clear that the decline in church membership for most regional associations was a long-term trend, leaders did what leaders in mono-optional cultures always do to maintain the status quo: look for bright spots. They found it in the financial sky. While membership was down, the per capita giving was going up! We were not actually losing members who were really members; we were shedding deadwood; we were gaining commitment!

What was actually happening is what happens as any mono-optional culture begins to break down. During its heyday it has accumulated a number of assets with fixed operational costs. It has also become accustomed to a certain standard of living that it does not want to lose. So when the call for what it has to offer begins to decline it actually raises the price.[37] This has been the case in denominational churches with their members. Anyone with a listening ear has heard the growing complaint among church members that no one really cares to contact them until the fall stewardship campaign.

But this has clearly been the case with regional associations. Many regional associations are funded by local congregations and the funding formula is often calculated on the number of members in the congregation or its revenue, or both. As membership and local church revenue has dropped, regional associations have adjusted their formulas upward to stave off the impact. In some situations, nearly 25 percent of local church revenue is siphoned off to support the regional association.

This effort of a mono-optional culture to keep revenue constant by increasing the price of the service is only a temporary fix. Eventually the financial pressure passed down the line merely accelerates the decline. Finally, the institutions face the choice of either shifting toward a servant culture or dying as a mono-optional one. Many churches have made or are making this shift. They are helping members of this very commodity-based culture recover their souls. They are reaching a new generation of Christians, not with the message of institutional obligation, but with the message of serving Jesus in his Kingdom.

Unfortunately, local churches are making this shift faster than regional associations. Their appeals to local churches based on institutional loyalty are now falling on the ears of those who are more oriented to a servant culture. They are asking the question: "What case can you make for how you will use the money from this church? Tell us whom you are serving?"

I was a pastor for 20 years and I have to say that I did not really learn to raise money until I became the executive director of a Christian nonprofit. When you are the pastor of a church, it is relatively easy to use the authority of Scripture to make the claim that God requires people to support the ministry of the church. Unfortunately, if a church is still exhibiting a mono-optional culture, it often doesn't feel the need to really make the case that this church is your best investment to impact the world for the Kingdom of God. If a regional association is still exhibiting a mono-optional culture, it often doesn't feel the need to make the case that this regional association is your best investment for providing what you need to become a vital, effective congregation.

As redeveloped regional associations shift to servant cultures, they can learn from the nonprofit community how to do servant-based fund raising. I want to sketch out what this looks like.

Servant-Based Fundraising

In servant-based fundraising you are focused on serving your donors. Donors are persons who have resources for a mission in the world. You are offering a service to them by providing an opportunity for their mission to find concrete expression through the giving of their resources. This is a transformational experience; both the giver and the receiver are enriched in the experience because it is grounded in a spiritual impulse. If the donor merely has resources and no mission in the world, then he or she is reduced to a commodity in a pure business sense and whatever is offered is purely transactional. The donor is not changed or enriched in the process. If a person buys a raffle ticket to support the youth ministry because she has a heart for youth, she is a partner with you in ministry.

Servant-based fundraising is liberating because it does not reduce the leader to an attitude of begging or apology. Servant-based fundraising is based upon the principle that your donor needs you as much as you need him or her. Imagine for a moment that you had a person with an environmental mission in his heart to care for God's creation, but no organizations existed for carrying out that mission. Most people do not have the time, nor the talent, to create such an organization from scratch. Without the organization's existence, the expression of the donor's mission, and to some extent God's purpose for his life would be thwarted.

This concept was extremely helpful for me. As a pastor, I carried the typical reticence that pastors have in dealing with the issue of financial giving. It was liberating for me in my nonprofit work to realize that by inviting persons to give to Montaña de Luz, I was actually offering them a gift as well: an avenue for concretely expressing their values in the world. This introduced an element of mutuality into the conversation. As a person asking for support to the project, I was not coming from below the person, as if they were doing me a favor. Neither was I coming from above the person, as if I was the only legitimate option for their giving. With this understanding it was an exchange that was truly transformational.

Contrast this with mono-optional-based fundraising that is characterized by

- Exclusivity — We are the sole legitimate option for your giving;

- Assessment — We are not going to demonstrate why you should give to us, we are merely going to inform you of the amount you owe;

◆ Beggar mentality — We hate to keep asking you, but we cannot survive unless you do something to help us.

Servant-based fundraising has two eyes. It keeps one on the needs of the donor and one on the mission. It makes its case based on the five reasons that people give to anything:

Pattern of giving — People tend to be consistent in the pattern of ministries they support because the basic missional orientation of their heart is consistent. You best serve people by providing them with giving opportunities that connect to longstanding, deeply held concerns. A person on a church board (your customer) may not have a pattern of giving to denominational causes, but they may have a commitment to family ministry. Servant-based fundraising will connect your appeal to that set of values.

Reciprocity — People give to ministries when they also receive something they value in return. If this is purely transactional (for example, to win a raffle prize), then your donor has been reduced to a commodity. But this is not always the case. It is legitimate for a church board to make a contribution with the promise of training from the regional association to become a more vital church because there is the expectation of transformation — on both sides.

Peer giving — People give to ministries when they know that other persons they respect are also giving. This is because donors have two needs: reassurance and community. Donors need reassurance that they are making a good choice when making a substantial contribution. Donors, like everyone else, want to be part of a community of people who are sharing their experience. Church board members want to know that other church board members they respect are ready to make a substantial gift. They also want to know that the boards of other churches they respect are making substantial gifts as well.

Values — People give to ministries when those ministries address core values in their lives. In the church, these are the values of the Kingdom. It cannot be assumed that church boards know or believe that the core values of the Kingdom are being addressed by the regional association, and addressed in a way that is preferable to their own local expression as a congregation. The case has to be made.

Limited opportunity — People are drawn to giving opportunities that are unique or limited in time. When the church is effective in it mission, donors realize that there is no other organization quite like the church. There are many worthy agencies engaged in wonderful missions. However, the church addresses the spiritual needs of persons in a way that is unique. Church boards have a pattern of commitment to the uniqueness of the Christian mission. Regional associations need to make the case that they are fostering and expanding that unique mission in a way that the local church alone cannot do. They also need to be able to make the case that they are the church board's best investment for consultant services should they need assistance.

If you look at this list and conclude that it is only about how to shape a marketing campaign, then you only have received half the message. First and foremost, this list should provide the criteria for evaluating your mission appeal in a servant, rather than mono-optional culture. Specifically you must ask

- Does what my regional association offers connect with the pattern of giving in my church boards and issues that have been of importance to their members over the years (including new, non-cradle members)?

- Does my regional association provide the services that are most important to them, that is, resources that help them become vital, effective churches?

- Have we built a solid base of support from a wide range of churches and board leaders who express confidence in what the regional association is doing and the worthiness of its support?

- Can we make the case that what the regional association is doing clearly enacts Kingdom values and does so in a way that the local church cannot do alone?

- Can we make the case that the ministry of the regional association is uniquely valuable and provides services we can't find anywhere else?

When we look at the information derived from surveys of over 1,200 persons, three issues emerge. First, it appears that in many cases the assessment of churches by regional associations is perceived as an *obstacle* to their own local fundraising. This coincides with the plea of many church boards to help them make the case with their members that the regional association is a legitimate destination for a portion of their revenue. Regional associations not only need to make the case for giving to the regional association with their customer, the church board, they also need to equip that board to make a convincing case with church members.

Second, as we look at the priorities that respondents indicate for their regional associations, they seem to be out of alignment with the resource allocation of those bodies. Simply put, governing boards are wondering what value they are getting for their money on things they really care about. This leaves the regional association even more vulnerable on controversial issues that may have little to do with congregational vitality. Issues become a focal point for the dissatisfaction regarding the general lack of services that the regional association is providing on matters that really count.

Finally, the research suggests that for many church boards, a factor in deciding how much they give to the regional association (in voluntary situations) is the perceived efficiency of the operation. They are not sure if the overhead expenses are appropriate or not. Many tend to be skeptical.

This brings us to the question of the funding of transformational regional associations and how to reestablish their credibility as a legitimate destination for local church revenue, the subject of the next chapter.

Discussion Questions

For church members and leaders

1. What are the three top reasons you give money to your church?

2. What are the three top reasons your church gives money to your regional association?

3. What case does your regional association make to your church leaders that your financial contribution is an excellent financial investment in the Kingdom of God?

For regional associations

1. Would you say that your regional association functions as a mono-optional culture or a multi-optional (servant) culture when it comes to fundraising? What leads you to your conclusion?

2. What case does your regional association make to your church leaders that your financial contribution is an excellent financial investment in the Kingdom of God?

3. Evaluate your regional association's fundraising approach using the criteria found on page 144.

Chapter Seventeen

STRUCTURING REVENUE

A budget, like poetry, makes the invisible appear.[38]
— adapted from Nathalie Sarraute

If you are struggling with the line of reasoning in the book so far, this next chapter may be especially difficult. Even if you have followed the line of reasoning in the book and are comfortable with it so far, this next chapter will be especially difficult.

During one of my childhood family vacations, my parents bought a souvenir cup that said, "Money isn't everything. But it's way ahead of whatever is in second place."

Then there is this little gem: "When someone says, 'it's not the money; it's the principle of the thing!' ... it's the money."

Nonetheless, I am going to pretend that it is the principle of the thing and use those principles to shape a conversation around the funding of regional associations.

Principle #1: The health and vitality of congregations is the first priority of regional associations.

This suggests that we should shape the resources offered to congregations around their needs. Congregations have three basic needs: consultant services, regulatory services, and collective action (see Table 17.1).

Regulatory services are those basic functions required to preserve law and order within the particular polity. These include establishing standards for admission, setting procedures for discipline and dismissal, managing fiduciary responsibilities, and insuring adherence to a particular polity.

Consultant services are those discretionary services that a church needs which require skills that do not lie within the congregation. Consultant services include facilitation, subject-matter expertise, and training.

Table 17.1. How Different Functions Are Dealt with in Organizations

Function	*Regulatory*	*Consultant Services*	*Collective Action*
Evaluated by	Quality control	Value added	Overhead
Pricing	Basic assessment	Fee for service	Mission contribution
Requires	Consistency/Accuracy	Subject-matter expertise	Collaborative skill
Driven by	Political necessity	Organizational need	Opportunity
Structure	Hierarchy	Horizontal	Board
Type of business	Ecclesiastical	For profit/Nonprofit	Nonprofit

Collective action is the combination of resources from a number of different organizations to accomplish a particular mission. This might include food pantries, Christian schools, advocacy ministries, new church development, etc.

Principle #2: Services should be organized and staffed to provide the best service possible.

The challenge posed by the three functions is that they have different purposes and require different kinds of organizational structure and staffing. Let's take an example. Think about the staff of your local McDonald's. They are experts in delivering a meal quickly and customized to your particular order. They get it wrong occasionally. Did you get a chicken sandwich when you wanted a hamburger? No problem, they can get you a hamburger in 45 seconds. Do you mind that information about your order is flashed on a screen for everyone to see? Nope. The more visible the information, the better. Does it matter that the product lies out in the open for anyone to pick up? Actually, no. It makes things faster. Did your employee steal some of the product? No problem. A few French fries here or there don't make much difference anyway.

Now, try to imagine this same McDonald's crew running your local bank. Does it matter that they make mistakes? You bet! It can take a lot of time to clear up a bank error. Do you want all your account information flashed on a monitor visible in the lobby? Want a pickle with your identity theft claim? Do you mind if your money is thrown into bins until someone has the time to deliver it where it goes? Do you need to be concerned if an employee steals some of the money? You get the picture.

Now reverse it. Try to imagine your bank crew running your local McDonald's. Do you want the teller handling your entire transaction from cooking your hamburger to putting it on the bun to deep-frying the potatoes to pouring your drink, just to make sure it's right? Do you want your teller counting out the French fries to make sure they balance at the end of the day?

This is only a mildly exaggerated version of what happens when a regional association does not recognize the need to organize and staff its services differently depending upon the function. Mono-optional cultures tend to be driven by the regulatory function. They can move slowly because they don't have to worry about losing the customer; the customer has no other options. They also tend to be hierarchical with relatively small spans of control in the management positions, exactly what you want in a regulatory function.

Many denominational systems have retained a regulatory mentality that has engulfed all their functions. In the 1950s and 1960s, regional associations had a substantial number of resources that were generated by a relatively small amount of effort. The challenge was to regulate the flow of those resources to avoid a mistake. Today, the resources are more meager. However, the focus is still a regulatory one.

This works fine in areas where a mistake would be potentially catastrophic. It works poorly in situations that are opportunity-driven and fast action is required in a rapidly changing environment. Neither does it work well when a church is in urgent need of consultant services but the staff that might provide those services is tied up in regulatory functions. The leader of a regulatory function is very different from the leader of a stable of consultants, and that person is very different from the equivalent of a mission project (or nonprofit) executive director. And because they are so different, it is wise to keep them distinct in the organization. But there is another reason. Funding.

Principle #3: Services should be provided in the most cost-effective way possible.

There are a number of nonprofits in the world, large and small, that are an expression of collective action. These provide a whole host of services, some religiously based, some not, to persons in various kinds of need. These organizations make their case to churches, foundations, corporations, and individuals for support.

The research shows that people give to these causes because they resonate emotionally with the values of the donor. However, in making their decision, they generally will evaluate data regarding the project; for example, how the money is spent, the quality of the program, and the percent of income going to overhead. People are less likely to give to a project with a large percentage of the donation going to administration rather than direct service to the persons in need.

Every director of a nonprofit lives with this reality. I dealt with it by asking a few large donors with a strong commitment to the project to designate their contribution to overhead. This enabled me to say to other donors that one hundred percent of their gift was going to directly help HIV-infected children in Honduras. This information, along with an emotional tug from small children, made Montaña de Luz an extremely attractive giving opportunity.

Mission efforts (collective action) that are "owned" by a regional association should be required to function as independent profit and loss centers within the organization. They should make their pitch to congregations along with every other nonprofit in the world. Church boards should be encouraged to make their funding decisions based upon the appeal of the project to the values of the congregation, the quality of the program, and the percent of the donations spent on overhead.

If regional associations are going to "broker" the relationship between congregations and other nonprofits, they should indicate the cost of that service. If, for example, a regional association has a staff person for mission who works half-time and manages a mission portfolio of $50,000 that is collected from congregations and then allocated to those agencies, the church board should be advised how much it is costing for the regional association to serve as a pass-through agency. If the cost of a half-time position, including salary, benefits, office space, and other business expenses is $50,000, the church board should be advised of that cost and it should be added into the calculation of overhead.

If a regional association can provide a high-quality mission service that represents the collective effort of a significant number of congregations and is cost-effective, then it should have no problem winning the financial support of church boards compared to other similar mission projects in the world. If a regional association cannot do this, then it should not be levying a mandatory assessment on congregations to support a work that cannot hold its own as a free-standing service that church boards will support.

The funding of consultant services is yet a different matter. People buy consultant services because of the value they add to the organization.

Churches do not care what my overhead is for my business. They don't ask to see my business balance sheet. What they care about is how much value I am adding to their organization for the fee I am charging and how that compares with other consulting options. It is for this reason that I recommend that the consultant work of the regional association be split from any mission work. They are two different functions with two different staffing requirements and two different decision-making processes in the mind and heart of the customer.

A regional association should provide consultant services to its customers on a fee-for-service basis. Again, it should be able to make the case that it provides the best consultant services for the money available on the market today. It has the potential competitive advantage over other consultants in the field because of its expertise with its particular polity. It also has persons who are a known commodity to that community. By making these consultants available on a fee basis, a regional association also expands their potential market. There is nothing that would prevent effective consultants serving one regional association from serving others as well. The result would be a higher quality of service offered to churches only as they need the service.

In this model, mandated assessments for resourcing church boards would be eliminated. If the consultant wants to provide the equivalent of a service policy with an annual fee, that decision would be left to the consultant and the church. In that case, unexpected needs like pastoral transition services would be available when they arise.

If regional associations cannot sustain consultant services on a fee basis, they should leave that business to others. One option is outsourcing. Let's say that a regional association has a staff person that it is paying $100,000 to provide consultant services for its church boards. It could choose to totally outsource this work to an independent contractor. It would have no responsibility for office space, business expenses, or support staff. The relationship could be easily terminated or modified. There would be much less entanglement with bystander issues.

Another option would be for a regional association to establish themselves as a referral network to consultant services that they have vetted and can endorse. This network can be managed by a staff member who is hired to add or remove vendors, conduct evaluations, and facilitate the linking of church boards to resources. Since this arrangement serves as a promotional service for consultants and saves them marketing dollars, they should be willing to pay a referral fee back to the regional association for the privilege of placement on the network.

If a regional association chooses to hire a network manager, it could probably do that with a quarter-time position working from home, maybe $25,000. If the assessment from congregations was cut by $80,000, they could use the money they saved on consultants in the network. If the referral fee were 20 percent, the regional association would create a revenue stream of $16,000. Overall the regional association would have $36,000 in additional revenue with additional expenses of $25,000. And it would be providing a larger range of resources.

The reader might argue that the church boards can't afford to pay for consultant services even with a reduction in their assessment. But if that is the case, then the regional association can't afford to pay for them either, a fact that is hidden in the mandatory assessment process. It is far better to create transparency on this issue with a network of consultants than to pretend that there is enough money to do everything if only the regional association were better managed.

This approach represents my best thinking at restoring the credibility of regional associations. By charging only for mandated regulatory functions (no cheating here by sliding in other items!) it provides crystal transparency on those essential costs. It is equivalent to paying for a police department, judicial system, and secretary of state. These are simply the costs of being a community.

By putting collective action and consultant services on a competitive footing with other providers, you are respecting the capacity of church boards to make the best decisions for what they need. You are ultimately freeing yourself from the burden of having to justify the services you are providing through a mandatory assessment while providing quality options for their growth and service to the world.

Discussion Questions

For church members and leaders

1. What are your thoughts regarding the current system of funding your regional association?

2. If you had a choice, what services would you "buy" from your regional association? What services would you "buy" from other providers?

3. If you had a choice for where to invest your mission dollars, what would be your priorities?

For regional associations

1. How satisfied are you with the current process for funding your regional association?

2. What regulatory, consultant, and mission functions does your regional association currently perform?

3. What do you think would happen if regulatory, consultant, and mission functions were split out into separate revenue streams that were funded in different ways?

Chapter Eighteen

GETTING STARTED

Whatever you can do,
or dream you can do, begin it.
Boldness has genius,
power and magic in it.[39]
— Goethe

My wife is the director of a hospital emergency department. She took her current assignment about three years ago. She then set about the task of shifting the culture of the department from an internally focused, technically driven organization to an externally focused, service-driven organization. In doing so, she joined thousands of leaders in the world today who are working hard to shift their organizations to be more effective in their mission. This book is calling regional associations to the same task. We are not alone. We must not feel sorry for ourselves.

At the beginning of her work we would often talk about the enormousness of the task. I would remind her that she was in a marathon, not a sprint, and that the shift she was trying to make would take three to five years to accomplish. Now, three years into it, I would say she is right on course. It helps to be realistic about how long a process will take.

The ideas proposed in this book do not represent a quick fix. They will require at least ten years to implement, perhaps an entire generation. The church of the twenty-first century will require a different support structure if it is to impact the world in a transforming way. We are talking about an organizational reformation. The journey of a century begins with what you will do today.

Every context is different, so it is impossible to lay out a detailed plan for how changes should take place. The purpose of this final chapter is to lay out a broad process as a starting point.

First, it will be important for you as a leader to understand where your regional association is now. Having a transformation vision statement is a good beginning, but it is only that. The assessment found in Table 18.1 on page 156 could be useful.

Second, develop a core of leaders who understand what a transformational regional association is and what a redevelopment process involves. Begin by gathering together a group of leaders to discuss this book.

I would encourage church leaders to have conversations with the leaders of other organizations in their communities that have had to make substantial cultural shifts to see what they can learn from them. This would include other nonprofits as well as for-profit organizations. Talk with the leaders of libraries, hospitals, banks, human service and charitable organizations, hotels, zoos, and science centers as a starting point. Put together an association-wide symposium on shifting organizational culture. This will not only promote learning, it will strengthen the relationship between your churches and the other organizations in your community.

Third, the leadership core will need to engage the association in a change process. This will require shifting perspective from an internal, mono-optional focus to an external, multi-optional focus. Engaging leaders from other organizations will help with this process. Your association will need to craft a case for change (purpose), and a vision for the future (picture).

Fourth, it will be necessary for the formal leadership of the association to make the decision to redevelop the association using whatever process the polity requires. The vision of a transformational association focused on developing healthy, vital congregations, will need to be adopted. This is a major decision. People will need to be given information regarding what it will look like, but they also will need to understand it is a discovery process. The future will unfold as the Spirit leads.

Fifth, a long-range planning process with broad participation will need to be engaged. It should identify critical success factors, establish strategic targets, set annual goals, and generate tasks with accountability. This work will probably need to be facilitated by an outside resource.

We engage this process as the work of the Gospel. It can only be sustained under the inspiration, guidance, and strength of the Holy Spirit. As we said in the beginning, the goal is not to make life easier by eliminating problems, it is to make life richer by addressing higher problems.

I'm told that if you take the Pali Highway northbound out of Honolulu, you'll discover something that a lot of people who have never been to Hawaii found out long ago. When you get to the Pali Pass, turn right on Park Street. Go one block and you come to Easy Street. Turn left and go one more block. There you'll see a sign that says Dead End.

This is not Easy Street. This is the road less traveled.

Table 18.1. Transformational Regional Association Assessment

Vision

❑ We have a transformational vision statement.

Communication

❑ We have a clear, concise case for change.

Values

❑ Our leaders have a clear understanding and commitment to indirect success.
❑ We have shaped our meetings and organizational units to reflect the value of indirect success.
❑ Our leaders demonstrate a high value for strategic engagement with member churches.
❑ Our leaders demonstrate a high value for developing leaders.
❑ Our leaders demonstrate a high value in linking members to the direction of the denomination.

Skills

❑ Our leaders are serving effectively as strategic coaches.
❑ Our leaders have a working menu of strategic options for churches.
❑ Our leaders are skilled at allocating resources to serve the vision.
❑ Our leaders are skilled at uncovering opportunities.

Time Allocation

❑ Our leaders have allocated their time to reflect the strategic priorities of the regional association.
❑ Our leaders practice strategic deferral.

Warning Signs

❑ Our leaders are not engaging in or creating direct-success activities.
❑ Our leaders are not creating parish-type activities at the level of the regional association.
❑ Our leaders are not engaged in excessive travel beyond the regional association.
❑ Our leaders are not engaged in excessive involvement in community or national issues.

Culture

❑ We clearly function as a multi-optional culture.
❑ We are externally focused.
❑ Generally we realize that local church leaders have other options and that we must make our case.
❑ Our staff members provide excellent service to churches requesting help or support.

Customers, clients, bystanders

❑ We are clear who our customers are.
❑ We are clear who our clients are.
❑ We are clear who our bystanders are.
❑ We set our priorities based upon our customers' needs.
❑ We have a systematic way of determining our customers' needs.
❑ We have a comprehensive strategic resourcing plan for each church.
❑ We have a consistent method for evaluating how we are performing for those we serve.

Developing leaders

Our leadership development approach is
❑ Systematic
❑ Focused on core competencies
❑ Reproducible
❑ "Just in time"
❑ High-quality
❑ Strategically aligned
❑ Onsite when possible
❑ Uses adult learning principles
❑ Focused on what pastors need ("The Pretty Dozen")

Fundraising and Revenue Structure

❑ We focus on our customers' needs when asking for money.
❑ We can and do demonstrate
  ❑ Value added
  ❑ Low overhead
  ❑ Quality control

Appendix A

THE DATA SETS

This book is based on a number of data sets that have been collected over approximately 30 years. Descriptions of those data sets are found below:

The Church Assessment Tool ©

This instrument is an 85-question survey administered to congregations for purposes of strategic planning, transition planning, and succession planning. It was used in a pilot project of the Episcopal Church in 2006–2007. There are now approximately 80 churches in the database including Episcopal, Protestant, denominational, and non-denominational churches. (See Appendix B.)

The Church Planning Questionnaire ©

This instrument is an earlier version of the *Church Assessment Tool*. It was created in the late 1970s by Dr. Grayson Tucker from Louisville Presbyterian Seminary. Over 400 churches from many denominations, in every setting, and of every size have used this survey.

Standing on the Banks of Tomorrow

A study conducted by Carolyn Weese in 1992 and 1993 for seven seminaries seeking to understand how to improve their educational program. On-site interviews of 91 pastors and telephone interviews of another seven pastors were conducted. Churches were located throughout the United States. The data is an important collection of information regarding the educational needs of clergy in mid-size, large, and mega-churches. (See Appendix C.)

The Passion-Effectiveness Tool ©

An instrument developed in response to a request from Pittsburgh Presbytery to provide a tool for clergy candidates matching the categories found in the *Church Assessment Tool*. The survey seeks to measure both interest in a particular area of the life of a church as well as capacity to function well. It also gauges future interest, theological orientation, and preferred organization flexibility. Fifty-five pastors have participated in the project to date.

The Regional Association Assessment Tool ©

This instrument was developed to assess attitudes and behavior of churches' leaders toward their regional association. It generates a series of performance indices, goals for the future, as well as drivers of satisfaction, participation, and giving (where appropriate). It also provides a set of priorities for the future. It is appropriate for regional associations engaged in strategic or succession planning.

The Regional Association Staff Assessment Tool ©

An instrument developed to assess the attitudes and behaviors of staff members in regional associations toward their work and work environment. The report generates a series of performance indices on morale, teaming, conflict management, general management, professional and personal development, and client difficulty. It also provides a set of priorities for the future and drivers of satisfaction. It is appropriate for staff development as well as strategic and succession planning.

The Patron Assessment Tool ©

An instrument developed to assess the attitudes and behaviors of community members toward their public libraries. It is useful for strategic, tactical, and marketing development.

The Staff Assessment Tool ©

An instrument developed to assess the attitudes and behaviors of library staff members toward their work and work environment. It is appropriate for staff development as well as strategic and succession planning.

Appendix B

THE REGIONAL ASSOCIATION ASSESSMENT TOOL

Important Metrics of Organizational Health
by J. Russell Crabtree

> *This questionnaire can give the leadership of a regional association important baseline information on the health of the organization. It can be used for strategic planning or in shaping a leadership search.*

The Report

A. **Key Indicators**

   Overall Satisfaction

   Engagement Trends

   Top Three Priorities for the Future

   Priorities for the Primary Leader

B. **Drivers**

   Satisfaction

   Engagement

C. **Critical Success Factors**

D. **Comprehensive Priority Set**

E. **Priorities Sorted by Group**

F. **Performance Dashboard**

G. **Performance Indices**

   Hospitality Index

   Program Support Index

   Decision Making Index

   Personal Engagement Index

   Flexibility Index

   Morale Index

   Conflict Management Index

ASSESSMENT QUESTIONS

As we prepare to search for the next [Senior Leader] of our [Regional Association], our leaders want to know what you think about our work together. We are interested in your honest views and beliefs in a variety of areas. In this instrument, you will find statements about how you see things related to our [Regional Association]. We also want to know what you believe should receive more energy in the future. Finally, we need to know some things about you and you will find questions designed to help us understand you better.

This survey is to be filled out by active and retired clergy, boards, and members of working groups within our [Regional Association]. Please do not discuss the questions with one another prior to completing the questionnaire.

In each case, *your* impressions, feelings, and opinions are important for [Regional Association] planning. In some cases, you may feel that your opinions are not well informed. Please go ahead and give your impression as it is now, even though you realize it could change by talking with others. Use the "Don't Know" response only in those rare cases where you have no impression at all.

I. Your Perspectives

In the blank by each of the following statements, write the number from the scale that best expresses your view:

1	2	3	4	5	6	7
Strongly Disagree	Disagree	Tend to Disagree	Tend to Agree	Agree	Strongly Agree	Don't Know

_____ 1. The [Regional Association] makes available policies and procedures that are helpful in the day-to-day operation of a church.

_____ 2. I experience a high level of collegiality as members of the [Regional Association] work together.

_____ 3. The leaders of our [Regional Association] show a genuine concern to know what people are thinking when decisions need to be made.

_____ 4. The [Regional Association] has done a good job of developing a shared vision that unites us.

_____ 5. The members of the [Regional Association] exhibit a genuine hospitality toward one another and new persons entering our [Regional Association] community.

_____ 6. There is frequently a small group of members that opposes what the majority want to do.

_____ 7. Members have discovered that involvement in the work of the [Regional Association] can be a source of energy and spiritual renewal.

_____ 8. Problems between groups in this [Regional Association] are usually resolved through mutual effort.

_____ 9. The [Regional Association] is effective in recognizing trends in the larger society and in helping us adapt in order to deal with those changes.

_____ 10. Most important decisions about what the [Regional Association] should do are really made by the same, small group of people.

_____ 11. In important decisions in our [Regional Association], adequate opportunity for consideration of different approaches is usually provided.

_____ 12. As a [Regional Association] we do a good job communicating with one another in a way that keeps us aware and engaged.

_____ 13. Our [Regional Association] does a good job helping each member understand that he or she has an important role to play.

_____ 14. Our [Regional Association] does a good job supporting persons who are serving in various [Regional Association] ministries.

_____ 15. A positive spirit exists between the leaders of my congregation and the [Regional Association].

_____ 16. In this [Regional Association] it seems to me that we are just going through the motions. There isn't much excitement about it among our members.

_____ 17. The [Regional Association] has been successful in helping congregations like mine become more vital and effective.

_____ 18. Some leaders in my congregation have unresolved issues with the [Regional Association] that get in the way of our working together.

_____ 19. I find [Regional Association] meetings to be a good use of my time and energy.

_____ 20. On the whole, I am satisfied with how things are in our [Regional Association].

_____ 21. Among most of the members of our [Regional Association] there is a healthy tolerance of differing opinions and beliefs.

_____ 22. I trust the [Regional Association] to provide strong and competent support to my congregation during challenging times such as changes in clergy or other transitions.

_____ 23. The [Regional Association] has been a valuable resource in helping my congregation cultivate the financial giving of our people.

_____ 24. Because of my involvement in the [Denomination], I feel clearer about God's purpose for my life than I did three years ago.

_____ 25. Our [Regional Association] helps members become engaged by finding roles for people that fit their gifts.

_____ 26. Our [Regional Association] tends to stay very close to established ways of doing things.

_____ 27. There is a disturbing amount of conflict in our [Regional Association].

_____ 28. Our [Regional Association] provides adequate opportunities for members to engage in work that is meaningful.

_____ 29. Persons who serve as leaders in our [Regional Association] are generally representative of the members.

_____ 30. The whole spirit in our [Regional Association] makes people want to get as involved as possible.

II. About the Future

In this section of the assessment, possible goals are listed for our [Regional Association] in the next three to five years. The leaders of the [Regional Association] are interested in knowing where you believe *additional* energy needs to be applied to expand or improve our work. If you believe that some ministries require *additional* energy because they are important and need to be expanded or improved, then you would give these a higher score. If you believe that other ministries require little or no *additional* energy because they are already being performed at an appropriate level of quality, then you would give these a lower score. Using the scale below, respond to the questions that follow:

1	2	3	4	5	6
No additional energy	Little additional energy	Moderate additional energy	Substantial additional energy	High additional energy	Don't Know

_____ 31. Equip congregations to be more effective in addressing problems affecting their surrounding communities.

_____ 32. Take a leadership role in new church development in promising regions of the [Regional Association].

_____ 33. Work with local congregations to increase the awareness of the [Regional Association]'s mission and its unique impact upon the region that it serves.

_____ 34. Provide on-site stewardship consultants and programs to local churches in order to substantially increase the financial resources of congregations.

_____ 35. Improve the programmatic resources that the [Regional Association] makes available to congregations to insure that they are the most effective ways to do ministry in the church today.

_____ 36. Streamline the [Regional Association] organizationally and administratively so that it makes better use of financial resources.

_____ 37. Cultivate a more consistent hospitality and develop a higher level of trust within the [Regional Association].

_____ 38. Take a leadership role in working with churches that have completed their mission in a community and need to close.

____ 39. [LOCAL QUESTION]

____ 40. Equip pastors and other leaders in congregations with strategies that enable them to reach new members.

____ 41. Provide church leaders with the kinds of interpretive resources that will build more support for the work of the [Regional Association] among members of the congregation.

____ 42. Make the [Regional Association] more responsive to requests for assistance in dealing with particular needs including pastoral transitions, capital issues, or other pressing concerns.

____ 43. [LOCAL QUESTION]

____ 44. Develop a discernment process to rethink how to be vital [DENOMINATION] churches in our specific region.

____ 45. Deepen our spiritual capacity as congregations to respond to life with serenity, confidence, and hope.

____ 46. Equip pastors and other leaders in congregations to help members become growing, vital disciples.

III. Qualities of the Next [Senior Leader] of Our [Regional Association]

Below you will find a list of six qualities for the next [Senior Leader] of our [Regional Association]. We realize that each of these qualities is desirable, but we would like to know which are more important in your thinking and which are less important. Please RANK these six items from "1" to "6" with "1" meaning most important, "2" very important, "3" important, "4" somewhat important, "5" less important, and "6" least important. Each number should only be used once.

1	2	3	4	5	6	7
Most important	Very important	Important important	Somewhat important	Less	Least important	Don't Know

____ 47. An ability to work collaboratively with other members of the [Regional Association].

____ 48. A willingness to surround himself/herself with people who complement his/her weaknesses.

_____ 49. A capacity to oversee the fiscal affairs of the [Regional Association] in a way that makes the most of scarce resources.

_____ 50. An aptitude for developing and articulating a vision.

_____ 51. A knack for bringing out the best in people.

_____ 52. An ability to effectively encourage spiritual growth in others.

IV. Your Involvement

_____ 53. The role in which I am currently serving is

1	2	3	4
Active Clergy	Retired Clergy	[Regional Association] Committee/Commission	Board

_____ 54. I have been involved in this particular congregation

1	2	3	4	5	6
Less than 1 year	1–2 years	3–5 years	6–10 years	11–20 years	20+ years

_____ 55. Beyond going to [Regional Association] meetings, how engaged would you say that your church has been with any phase of the [Regional Association]'s life and work in the last 12 months?

_____ 56. Over the last three years how has your church's engagement with the [Governing Body] changed?

1	2	3	4
Less engaged	About the same	More engaged	Don't Know

_____ 57. If you have served in leadership of other [Denomination] churches, how would you compare your level of satisfaction with our current [Governing Body] to other [Governing Bodies] you have worked with?

1	2	3	4
Less satisfied here	About the same	More satisfied here	Not applicable

_____ 58. What would you say is your level of awareness regarding the work of the [Governing Body]?

1	2	3	4
Unaware	Somewhat aware	Moderately aware	Very aware

V. Information about You

____ 59. My gender is

1	2
Male	Female

____ 60. My age is

1	2	3	4	5	6	7
Below 19	19–24	25–34	35–44	45–54	55–64	65+

VI. Questions for Transition Planning

____ 61. It could take a number of months to call a new [Senior Leader]. As I think about my involvement in the [Governing Body] during that time I intend to be

1	2	3	4	5	6
Much less involved	Less involved	About the same	More involved	Much more involved	Don't know

____ 62. There are a number of additional responsibilities that may arise during this transition (for example, prayer, focus groups, committee work). Please indicate your level of availability to help with additional responsibilities as they arise:

1	2	3	4	5	6
Much less available	Less available	About the same	More available	Much more available	Don't know

____ 63. There are a number of additional financial costs during a transition (for example, search costs, relocation costs, etc.). Please indicate below what you believe your church's level of giving to the [Governing Body] should be during the transition.

1	2	3	4	5	6
Much lower giving	Lower giving	About the same	Higher giving	Much higher giving	Don't know

Appendix C

STANDING ON THE BANKS
OF TOMORROW

A Summary by Carolyn Weese

Description of the Research Project

On two occasions in 1991, at Glen Eyrie Conference Center in Colorado Springs, Colorado, Leadership Network drew together a group of senior pastors from large evangelical churches, and presidents, deans, and board members of seminaries. During the days they spent together, they discussed the large church, how the church in America is changing, and the type of leadership it takes to lead such a complex organism. They discussed what the seminary is offering for curriculum, the methods by which it is being taught, and whether the seminary graduate is adequately prepared to face the church of tomorrow.

At the end of the meetings, several seminaries contacted Leadership Network and said "we've heard enough to know that we need to hear more. How can we get information from the grass roots? Is there someone who can visit the mega-churches in our country in order to discover what their needs are so that we might shape what we do in order to produce a better end product?"

In January 1992, Carolyn Weese discussed the project with Bob Buford and Fred Smith. By March, seven seminaries were interested in this project, with others considering it. At that meeting, a study was designed within the following parameters:

1. The study would be limited to seven schools, in order to keep it from becoming too cumbersome. The seven schools in the project are Alliance Theological Seminary, Asbury Theological Seminary, Beeson Divinity School, Bethel Theological Seminary, Denver Seminary, Seminary of the East, and Western Seminary.

167

2. The seminaries equally would fund the project.

3. The study would be conducted and a written and verbal report would be presented to representatives of the seven schools. It would take place from July 1, 1992, through January 31, 1993.

4. Each school would be requested to supply a list of approximately 25 mega-churches that they would think of as a potential customer.

5. Each school also would be asked to send a statement of expectations from the study.

In June, Leadership Network mailed a letter to 146 senior pastors of large churches inviting them to participate in the project by granting a two-hour on-site interview. This two-hour block of time could be spent just with the senior pastor, or he could invite staff members to participate as well. In return, the church would receive a copy of the finished report.

One hundred and five responses were received from 23 states saying they would like to participate in the study. Trips were then plotted and appointments made. In the end there were:

91 On-site visits

 6 Interviews by phone

 3 Canceled the appointment and did not want phone interview

 3 Resigned their church and were unavailable

 2 Unavailable and did not want a phone interview

105 Total

Questionnaire Responses

The data in the questionnaire has been condensed and compressed and is offered as raw data with no explanation or amplification.

1. From your perspective, what do seminaries do well?

Biblical studies
Philosophy
Theology
Moral reasoning
Credential prospective pastors
Prepare academicians for graduate school

Ground students theologically

Church history

Languages

Prepare pastors for small, single-pastor parish setting.

Provide opportunity for personal interaction with leading academicians and theologians

Some give fair training in homiletics

Train pastors to teach and preach

Take money, provide employment for professors, give consistent theological view

Enhance one's critical thinking

Teach how to stick it out in a "small" church (satisfied with maintenance)

They develop the "head"

Scholars and libraries

Research

Exegesis

Students are made aware of resources

Clarification of call

2. Conversely, what are seminaries not doing well?

Marketing leadership

Spiritual formation

Evangelism

Understanding culture

Training pastors

Training leadership

Teaching management

Teaching relational skills, and interpersonal relationships

Teaching strategic planning

Teaching sociological interpretation

Teaching administration

Extremely weak on the practical side of ministry in a church

Few teach preaching well

Weak at staying in touch with local churches

Preparing ministers for administering a church programmatically, developing the stewardship program, providing vigorous leadership in moving a congregation ahead.

They don't train people in small group leadership, church leadership, administration, worship, evangelism and outreach, how to develop lay leaders.

Too much theory; not enough in the practical hands-on area

Deepening of spiritual life of students

Understanding of spiritual growth and spiritual warfare

Providing relevant and practical teaching

Function from cultural vacuum — out of touch

Preparation to work with multiple staff

They do not train pastors to pastor churches for growth

They do not train pastors to lead large churches

Management skills

Professors are usually not in touch

Not globally connected

Helping students to be street-wise and culturally relevant

They are not equipping people to be able to function well as pastors at whatever level because the teachers are out of touch with what actually happens and the theory is too far removed from reality. They are also working on old models of education that do not relate to today's person. They have a basically academic model and people don't relate to that.

Seminaries do not prepare students well to relate with people, understand the implications of contemporary culture as it relates to methodology in ministry, and be a visionary leader. Because of the lack of practical experience on the part of the faculty, the student does not gain a great deal of "street smarts" from their mentors. They don't fail in the academics of their study. They fail in the wisdom of godly, insightful leadership. The student is able to conjugate nouns and parse verbs, but lacks the skill and finesse to exegete their own culture or be an effective change-agent with people.

They don't teach about the problems and passion of church people and how churches function.

Not in touch adequately with the rapid developments of the changing church of the '80s and '90s.

Teaching vision for ministry

I would have appreciated exposure to more pastors with vibrant ministries, training in biblical assertiveness, financing a ministry, leadership and sermon preparation.

Communication preaching

Instill courage to risk
Build character
Preparing families for church careers
Preparing ministers for committees, elder board meetings, or dealing with difficult individuals
No training in use of modern media

3. Specifically, what subjects need to be provided in order to develop your staff and equip lay leaders?

Leadership development
    Theology of church leadership
    Elder leadership
    Missions leadership
    Goal setting
    Vision development
    Organizational dynamics
    Administration
    Recruiting and motivating volunteers
    Lay governance training
    Multiple staff leadership
    Development of philosophy of ministry
    Time management
    Computer programming
    Marketing
    Stewardship
    Personnel management
    Financial practices
Interpersonal skills
    Conflict resolution
    Leader's personal and emotional growth
    Mentoring
    Communication
    Small group dynamics
    How to bring about change
    How to deal with difficult people
    Personality development
    Managing marriage and ministry
    Ethical issues
    Development of devotional life

Cross-cultural communications
Crisis intervention
Counseling skills
Spiritual gifts and ministry
Core academics
Foundational Christian doctrine
Bible
Theology
Church history
Spiritual formation
Hermeneutics
Apologetics
Discipleship
Evangelism
Soul-winning
Building Christian community
Counseling
Church growth
Missions
Christian Education
Camping
Youth ministry
Children's ministry
Worship
Church planting

Needs of the Church

Throughout the interview process, senior pastors were asked what the seminary could do to help them meet the needs of their church. They were informed that the seminaries are interested in the big church as a market. Every pastor responded the same way. "We don't need anything from the seminary."

Considering that 55 of the 97 senior pastors have been in their present location ten years or longer, and most of the remaining 42 senior pastors have served other pulpits for a period of time, if they fail at what they are doing, it will not be because of something the seminary did or did not do. These senior pastors have scrambled throughout their career to obtain the tools that will assist them in building ministry. They realized early in their careers that their resources for leading and building a congregation would come from places other than the seminary. Their personal libraries contain large sections of "how to" books written by other churchmen, futurists, consultants, and those on the cutting edge of the church. They talk with their peers about what works and doesn't work. They attend conferences, workshops and seminars on timely topics. Not one person told me that they go back to the seminary for assistance. "Why should I? The seminaries are so far behind the church, they wouldn't understand what I am talking about!"

This feeling was the strongest in the largest churches and with the senior pastors having the most years of experience. It weakens to some extent as we slide down the size and tenure scale. However, even the Presbyterian group, who register the smallest in worship attendance and range from one to 20 years in the present location, reflected the same thinking.

My past experience tells me, if senior pastors of denominational churches were asked how the denomination could better assist them with their needs, the response would be the same.

When does the church need the seminary? What is the market? The market is not in the mid-size or large church today, but in the church of tomorrow. Every pastor said that we must have seminaries, but that seminaries must do a more complete job of preparing men and women for ministry. They are convinced, that if we were to eliminate seminaries, the church may remain solid and on track through this generation, but with each succeeding generation the theology would become weaker, disjointed, confused, and degenerate into "fluff and fuzz" religion.

The key is to develop and build today the leaders of tomorrow. The large church is on the rise in America, and these 97 churches are pleading for the seminaries to do a better job at preparing people for ministry. If the seminaries do not take this seriously, and do not take significant steps to move closer to the emerging church, there will be more and more churches developing their own mini-seminaries, institutes, Bible colleges, etc. The pattern is already established. If the need is not met, the church will try to meet it. If so, the orthodoxy of evangelical theology could be greatly compromised.

It is a common belief in most churches, except for the small ones, that seminaries prepare people to minister in small churches. The small churches think that the seminaries prepare pastors for large churches. Though this study was directed at the larger church, we must not lose sight of the smaller ones. In the next ten to 20 years, we will probably see a great many of the small churches close their doors. Part of this will be economics, as they simply cannot afford a pastor. Part of it will be that they have not been willing to change from straight traditional, mainline churches. They will last only as long as the present congregation can support them. It is doubtful that new people will join these fellowships.

I mention the small churches only because I believe that the ideas, thoughts and concepts that were communicated to me by the larger churches, in most cases, apply to the church of any size.

NOTES

1. Diarmund O'Murchu, *Quantum Theology: Spiritual Implications of the New Physics* (New York: Crossroad Publishing Company, 2004), 24.

2. John N. Williamson, ed., *The Leader-Manager* (San Francisco: John Wiley & Sons, 1986), 118.

3. Ibid., 261.

4. Clifton Kirkpatrick, *Perspectives* (Louisville, KY: Presbyterian Church USA, 2005), 1.

5. Charles Fulton, "Q&A: Context, analysis on Church membership statistics," Episcopal News Service Archive (2004), *www.episcopalchurch.org/3577_55181_ENG_HTM.htm*.

6. Cynthia Woolever, *Picture Your Presbytery Here* (Louisville, KY: Research Services, Presbyterian Church USA, 1999), 1.

7. Ibid., 1.

8. Kirkpatrick, *Perspectives*, 1.

9. Williamson, *The Leader-Manager*, 77.

10. Lawrence LeShan, *The Medium, the Mystic, and the Physicist: Toward a General Theory of the Paranormal* (New York: Penguin Group, 1974), 44.

11. Williamson, *The Leader-Manager*, 105.

12. Ibid., 144.

13. Ram Charan, Stephen Drotter, and James Noel, *The Leadership Pipeline: How to Build the Leadership-Powered Company* (San Francisco: John Wiley & Sons, 2001), 8.

14. Williamson, *The Leader-Manager*, 81.

15. Bryan Caplan, *The Myth of the Rational Voter: Why Democracies Choose Bad Policies* (Princeton, NJ: Princeton University Press, 2007), 182.

16. Rachelle Disbennett-Lee, *Definition of Coach, www.coachlee.com/whatis.htm*.

17. Ibid.

18. Liz Jazwick, Lecture at Nationwide Children's Hospital, Columbus, Ohio, 2006.

19. Williamson, *The Leader-Manager*, 244.

20. Sue Annis Hammond and Andrea B. Mayfield, *The Thin Book of Naming Elephants: How to Surface Undiscussables for Greater Organizational Success* (Bend, OR: Thin Book Publishing Company, 2004), 24.

21. Jay Conger and Beth Benjamin, *Building Leaders: How Successful Companies Develop the Next Generation* (San Francisco: Jossey-Bass Publishers, 1999), 13.

22. Carolyn Weese, "Standing on the Banks of Tomorrow," unpublished report, 1993.

23. Conger and Benjamin, *Building Leaders: How Successful Companies Develop the Next Generation,* 9.

24. Ibid., 253.

25. Lecture Notes, "How to Train Adults" (Kansas City, MO: Paget-Thompson, National Seminars Training Group, Rockhurst University Continuing Education Center, Inc., 1996).

26. Conger and Benjamin, *Building Leaders,* 131.

27. Williamson, *The Leader-Manager,* 95.

28. Ibid., 386.

29. Hammond and Mayfield, *Naming Elephants,* 48.

30. Neil Astley, ed., *Staying Alive: Real Poems for Unreal Times* (New York: Miramax Books, 2003), 58.

31. Williamson, *The Leader-Manager,* 417.

32. O'Murchu, *Quantum Theology,* 9.

33. Everett M. Rogers, *Diffusion of Innovations* (New York: Free Press, 1995), 18.

34. Thom A. Mayer and Robert J. Cates, *Leadership for Great Customer Service: Satisfied Patients, Satisfied Employees* (Chicago: Health Administration Press, 2004), 27.

35. Caplan, *The Myth of the Rational Voter,* 80.

36. Hammond and Mayfield, *Naming Elephants,* 12.

37. Ichak Adizes, *Corporate Lifecycles: How Corporations Grow and Die and What to Do About It* (Upper Saddle River, NJ: Prentice Hall, 1988), 78.

38. Astley, *Staying Alive,* 413.

39. Robert Bly, James Hillman, and Michael Meade, eds., *The Rag and Bone Shop of the Heart* (New York: HarperCollins Publishers, 1992), 235.

THE AUTHOR

J. Russell Crabtree is an Ohio native and graduate of The Ohio State University with a degree in engineering physics. He worked in research at the Eastman Kodak company for three years in the area of optics and electrostatic control systems. He left industry to attend seminary and served as a pastor for 20 years. In 1998, Russ founded and served for five years as the executive director of Montaña de Luz, a project providing hospice care for abandoned children with HIV/AIDS in Honduras. In the wake of Hurricane Mitch, he founded and directed Ohio Hurricane Relief for Central America. He is the co-founder and president of Holy Cow! Consulting which provides strategic planning, training, and organizational assessment. He also founded and directs BestMinds, a company specializing in awareness and intervention training for suicide and domestic violence. He has worked with cross-professional teams in counties with high suicide rates to develop prevention and intervention strategies; he helped shape the suicide prevention plan developed by the State of Ohio.

Russ has extensive experience in assisting organizations across the United States with strategic planning, mediation, customer surveys, and training. He has worked with many different kinds of organizations including churches, libraries, colleges, and an arboretum. He has developed training for organizations in strategic planning, conflict management, team-building, staff morale, customer service, and enhancing board function.

As a Presbyterian pastor, Russ served in small, mid-size, and large churches in New York and Ohio. In that role, he was active in his regional association (presbytery) and worked in the areas of strategic planning, energy conservation, human sexuality, church consultation, presbytery staffing, and administrative oversight. He has served as a consultant to presbyteries and the Episcopal Church at both the national and diocesan level in the areas of training, succession planning, conflict management, and congregational assessment.

He has developed congregational and regional association assessment tools and has maintained a substantial database on church characteristics and congregations of all sizes and contexts. He is the creator of the CSAT and RSAT which are staff assessment tools for larger churches and regional associations, as well as the Church Assessment Tool — CAT. He has developed a number of products for churches in transition. He co-authored a book with Carolyn Weese that was published in 2004 entitled *The Elephant in the Board Room: Developing a Pastoral Succession Plan for Your Church*. The concepts of this book have been incorporated in a workbook developed to assist church leaders in pastoral succession planning. Using these materials he has assisted some of the largest churches in the United States in developing succession plans.

Russ has recently become an associate member of People Management International and is working with them to develop a comprehensive resourcing system for congregations and regional associations. The goal is to link excellence in organizational and motivational assessment with high quality resources that will strengthen churches as expressions of the Kingdom of God.

His second book, *Mountain of Light, The Story of Montaña de Luz* was published in 2005. He is also writing a book on surviving suicidal thinking entitled *A Second Day*, which is scheduled for publication in 2008.

Russ has four children and lives with his wife, Shawn, in Columbus, Ohio.

For further information contact:

J. Russell Crabtree
Holy Cow! Consulting
PO Box 8422
Columbus, Ohio 43201
614-208-4090
russ@holycowconsulting.com
www.holycowconsulting.com